LEGAL ETHICS

An Annotated Bibliography and Resource Guide

Frederick A. Elliston
Senior Research Associate
Illinois Institute of Technology

Jane van Schaick
Executive Director
Chicago Research Institute

FRED B. ROTHMAN & CO.
Littleton, Colorado 80127

1984

Library of Congress Cataloging in Publication Data

ELLISTON, FREDERICK.
Legal ethics.

Includes index.
1. Legal ethics—United States—Bibliography.
I. Van Schaick, Jane. II. Title.
KF305.A1E43 1984 016.174'3'0973 84-11599
ISBN 0-8377-0545-2

Printed in the United States of America

CONTENTS

ACKNOWLEDGMENT

We would like to thank several people and organizations for their help in compiling this bibliography. To Terrence O'Neil goes our thanks for many hours of labor at the Albany Law School Library; to Karen McLaughlin our appreciation for patience and forbearance in the many revisions of the manuscript; to Phillip McFarland and Donna Reid of the Center for the Study of Ethics in the Professions at the Illinois Institute of Technology our thanks for many details in the text and index; to the helpful staff of the Schenectady Public Library our admiration for the many items they miraculously obtained for us; to our publisher for their confidence in our ability to complete this project; and finally to Katrina and Holly van Schaick for their understanding in letting us and this work be.

LIST OF ABBREVIATIONS

ABA	American Bar Association
ABF	American Bar Foundation
ALI	American Law Institute
LSP	Legal Services Program
NAACP	National Association for the Advancement of Colored People
OEO	Office of Equal Opportunity
SEC	Securities and Exchange Commission

PREFACE

This monograph is intended as a reference guide for teachers of professional responsibility and legal ethics, legal scholars and philosophers conducting research on the practice of law. Over the past decade concern in the legal community for the ethics of lawyers has grown -- partly under the impetus of Watergate and the chiding of the Chief Justice, Warren Burger, to put their house in order. Lawyers are highly visible in our culture, occupying prominent positions in both government and business, yet they are held in low esteem by the public at large. Legal ethics is one effort to measure up to the standards of a profession.

This field has come to attract the attention of other academics, notably philosophers working in the emerging discipline of professional ethics. Typically their interest is much broader than the Code or Rules. Practices, such as plea bargaining and moral character and fitness tests raise serious ethical questions whether they are just and fair. Accordingly, this bibliography is much broader in scope than the issues raised by the Model Rules.

It is divided into three main sections: legal materials, topical materials and related materials. Abstracts are provided on articles, books and some films on lawyers' professional responsibility. The citations included, although not comprehensive given the exponential growth in the literature, nevertheless are representative of what has been published to date in the following selective categories: codes and discussions of professional responsibility; law school materials; lawyers' roles; law as a business; evidence; the courts; lawyers and special groups; philosophical materials; popular books; bibliographic materials; and historical works.

The first section focuses on the literature, mostly by lawyers, on professional responsibility and legal education. Much of the discussion centers around the Model Rules of Professional Conduct. Among others, notable authors like Monroe Freedman, Robert Kutak and Geoffrey Hazard are cited. Legal ethics as a general topic is also treated in this section.

Specific ethical issues are dealt with in the second section on topical materials. Familiar texts on the professional responsibilities of lawyers are listed as well as discussions of the role of law schools in the teaching of legal ethics. This section is subdivided into three parts: Lawyers' Role, Law as a Business and the Courts. Material on roles in general are listed as well as advocacy, the lawyer-client relationship, conflict of interest, public interest, corporate and government practice, the criminal justice lawyer, and lawyers' moral character. Lawyers, like other professionals, must run their practices as businesses. Advertising, distribution of services, regulation, and lawyers' relations to special groups are considered under this heading. The third subdivision on the courts is rich in ethical considerations involving judicial conduct, prosecutorial discretion, plea bargaining, disclosure, confidentiality and perjury.

The third section on related materials reviews the philosophical literature, popular books, historical material and bibliographies. It offers alternative perspectives on professional responsibility from outside the legal profession.

Finally, a listing of bar association addresses and telephone numbers is included for easy reference. An index of names refers the reader back to the author or editor. The table of contents and the index can be used together to facilitate quick reference.

Though we would like our work to be complete and authoritative, such a standard is ambitious for a dynamic field like legal ethics. Accordingly, we welcome suggestions for improving this bibliography in future editions.

FAE and JVS
Chicago, April 1984

PART ONE

LEGAL MATERIALS

CHAPTER ONE
PROFESSIONAL RESPONSIBILITY

A. CODES AND RULES

Abel, Richard L. "Why Does the American Bar Association Promulgate Ethical Rules?" Texas Law Review 59 (1981), 639-688.

Argues that professional ethics rules do not promote ethical behavior. Past and proposed codifications of ethical rules to guide the conduct of lawyers fail as norms because they are vague. The Model Rules Governing Professional Conduct are no improvement since they mandate in very general language conduct opposed to self-interest and then create numerous loopholes for those intent on evasion. The dilemmas to be resolved by the rules are inherent in the role of the lawyer and in liberal agnosticism about truth as embodied in the adversary system of justice.

Abramson, Elliott M. "Attorneys, Clients, 'Ethics'." Notre Dame Lawyer 52 (1977), 797-801.

Criticizes the Code of Professional Responsibility because it lacks an explicit description of a lawyer's obligations to justice, to assist the resolution of controversies and conduct his legal affairs in a manner promoting the truth. Abramson advocates stringent disclosure requirements and would forbid an attorney to advise a client to dissemble in order to avoid consequences of law which are clearly applicable.

American Bar Association. A Model Peer Review System. Chicago: American Bar Association, 1981.

Describes the American Bar Association's model for peer review of attorney competence, recommends evaluating attorney competence and suggests proceedings for incompetence and disciplinary peer review.

American Bar Association. National Center For Professional Responsibility. Code of Professional Responsibility by State. 2 volumes. Chicago: American Bar Association, 1981.

Compares the code of each state to the American Bar Association Model Code of Professional Responsibility. All differences are highlighted. These volumes help determine alternative approaches to ethical problems.

American Bar Association. Model Rules of Professional Conduct. Chicago: American Bar Association, 1983.

The Model Rules were adopted by the House of Delegates of the ABA on August 2, 1983. Topical areas discussed include: Client-Lawyer Relationship; Counselor; Advocate; Transactions with Persons other than Clients; Law Firms and Associations; Public Service; Information About Legal Services; and Maintaining the Integrity of the Profession.

American Bar Association. National Center For Professional Responsibility. Model Rules For Lawyer Disciplinary Enforcement. Chicago: American Bar Association, 1981.

The Standing Committee on Professional Discipline and the National Center for Professional Responsibility offer recommendations for use in drafting, updating and researching lawyer disciplinary rules.

American Bar Association. National Center For Professional Responsibility. Opinions on Professional Ethics. Chicago: American Bar Association, 1967.

This guide to answering ethical questions contains Ethics Committee Rule of Procedures, Annotated, and the Formal Opinions 1-315 of the Standing Coommittee on Professional Ethics issued 1924-1965. Informal opinions are included as part of the Canons of Professional Ethics, Annotated, and Canons of Judicial Ethics, Annotated. A citation to Formal and Informal Opinions is included that indicates whether an opinion has been followed, explained, modified or overruled in subsequent opinions.

"The American Bar Association's Retreat From Whistleblowing." Business Week (Aug. 31, 1981), p.56.

Discusses the American Bar Association's new draft of the revised lawyers' code of ethics that generally upholds longstanding rules requiring lawyers to keep client information secret. This draft reverses the previous controversial provision on whistleblowing.

American Bar Foundation. Annotated Code of Professional Responsibility. Chicago: American Bar Foundation, 1979.

Contains the text of the Code of Professional Responsibility along with historical notes, cross references to other sections of the Code and a summary of case law involving each section.

Block, Dennis J. and Barton, Nancy E. "Attorney's Responsibilities - Professional Ethics and the Federal Securities Laws." Securities Regulation Law Journal 8:4 (1981), 333-351.

Discusses the problems of corporate counsel and whether securities laws or professional ethics require the disclosure of facts constituting possible violations of securities law. SEC attempts to impose liability on attorneys under such circumstances. Discusses the Code of Professional Responsibility and proposed changes to forestall increased SEC regulation of corporate practice.

Brill, Howard W. "The Arkansas Supreme Court Committee on Professional Conduct 1969-1979: A Call For Reform." Arkansas Law Review 33 (1980), 571-722.

Describes the history and development of the Arkansas State Code of Professional Responsibility. Contains an indexed copy of the Code.

Brown, Louis S., and Harold G. Brown. "What Counsels the Counselor? The Code of Professional Responsibility's Ethical Considerations - A Preventive Law Analysis." Valparaiso University Law Review 10 (1976), 453-477.

Contend the Code's Ethical Considerations fail to address the role of the attorney as advisor. They distinguish the roles of the advocate and advisor and argue that the considerations must fully respond to the role of the attorney in society in order to impress upon all lawyers the ethical considerations which should buttress their professional conduct.

Cann, Wesley A. "Frivolous Lawsuits -- the Lawyer's Duty To Say 'No'." University of Colorado Law Review 52 (1981), 367-391.

Discusses the sources of a lawyer's duty to refrain from instituting frivolous law suits and the potential liability of a lawyer who does so. The duty to say "No" arises from the obligation to bring credit to the profession, to abide by specific provisions of the code and from the duty to uphold the legal system. Cann discusses the relevant provisions of the proposed Rules of Professional Conduct.

Carlin, Jerome E. Lawyers' Ethics: A Survey of the New York City Bar. New York: Russell Sage Foundation, 1966.

Reports the results of a survey of members of the New York City Bar to determine lawyers' attitudes toward ethical problems that arise in the practice of law. Carlin examines the social structure of the bar and attempts to relate status differences to ethical norms. He also examines attitudes towards client relations, contacts with the courts, government agencies and the organized bar. He describes the formal controls for professional discipline within the bar and lawyers' attitudes towards them.

Carrington, Paul. "The Major Problems of the Legal Profession during the Seventies." Southwestern Law Journal 30 (1976), 665-692.

Discusses major problems facing the legal profession in the 70's and the efforts of the ABA to deal with them. Topics include minimum standards of criminal justice; amendments to the Code of Professional Responsibility; anti-trust actions brought against the ABA; and the availability of legal services to the poor.

Comment. "The Lawyer's Moral Paradox." Duke Law Journal 1979 (1979), 1335-1358.

Argues that the Code of Professional Responsibility is commonly misperceived as an ethical code when it is in effect regulatory. It does not supplant the requirement for independent moral choice.

Cowger, Nancy. "Do Lawyers Really Need a Detailed Code of Ethics?" American Bar Association Journal 64 (1978), 522.

Argues that an overly detailed code of professional ethics is undesirable. The Canons of the Code of Professional Responsibility are adequate to inform attorneys of their responsibilities. More detailed and situation-oriented regulations should be the result of common law development, rather than a part of a code of ethics.

Finman, Ted and Theodore Schneger. "The Role of Bar Association Ethics Opinions in Regulating Lawyer Conduct: A Critique of the Work of the ABA Committee on Ethics and Professional Responsibility." University of California Los Angeles Law Review 29 (1981), 67-167.

Criticizes the informal opinions of the ABA's standing Committee on Ethics and Professional Responsibility, arguing that the committee's work is unsatisfactory because its procedures are non-adversarial. Committee members, as private practitioners, lack the time and initiative to uncover flaws in their colleagues' reasoning and do not base their opinions soundly on precedent. As a result the opinions offer a limited, one-sided view of complex problems and exert an unfortunate influence.

Frankel, Charles. "Review of the American Bar Association Code of Professional Responsibility." University of Chicago Law Review 43 (1976), 874-886.

Describes the Code and compares it with earlier codes. Frankel criticizes the Code because it is not embedded in an explicit examination of the issues raised by differences between professional and general ethical codes. It also fails to encourage non-adversary methods of dispute resolution and does not adequately address the changed circumstances of modern legal practice.

Freedman, Monroe H. "Are the Model Rules Unconstitutional?" University of Miami Law Review 35 (1981), 685-694.

Provisions of the Model Rules of Professional Conduct that would require a lawyer to reveal client confidences are attacked as an assault on the lawyer-client privilege and as violations of the Fifth and Sixth Amendments. Freedman advocates the American Lawyer's Code as an alternative.

Goebel, Roger J. "Professional Responsibility Issues in International Law Practice." American Journal of Comparative Law 29 (Winter 1981), 1-58.

Explores the responsibility of an American international lawyer serving foreign clients in the U.S. or American clients abroad. Potential conflict of interest problems for attorneys are more complex when the corporate client does business internationally. Duties owed to various levels of management and to shareholders are discussed, with special emphasis on counseling a client on the Foreign Corrupt Practices Act or corporate violations of foreign law.

Golec, Anthony M. "Legal Investigator and the Administration of Justice." Judicature 58 (1974), 134-136.

Describes the establishment of the National Association of Legal Investigators and the development of its strictly enforced code of ethics.

Green, Mark. "ABA [American Bar Association] as Trade Association." Verdicts on Lawyers eds. Ralph Nader and Mark Green. New York: Thomas Y. Crowell, 1976, 3-19.

Reviews the ABA's stance on socio-political issues from its founding in 1878 and finds that it has at times aligned itself with conservative forces and revealed a keen solicitude for its own public image rather than a concern for social issues. In the past decade the ABA has grown less stridently conservative and more modestly liberal. Green contends that although the ABA has shown increasing concern for the public interest, it has not yet moved away from a concern with its own well-being to a serious exploration of how its power could be used to advance the cause of legal justice.

Hazard, Geoffrey C. "How Far May a Lawyer Go In Assisting a Client in Legally Wrongful Conduct?" University of Miami Law Review 35 (1981), 669-683.

Examines the scope of D.R. 7-102(A)(7) of the Model Code of Professional Responsibility which forbids counsel to assist a client in illegal or fraudulent conduct. Hazard considers positive agency, tort and criminal law and asks whether they define forbidden conduct rather than the disciplinary rules of the Code.

Hodes, W. William. "The Code of Professional Responsibility, the Kutak Rules, and the Trial Lawyer's Code: Surprisingly, Three Peas in a Pod." University of Miami Law Review 35 (1981), 739-813.

Argues that the draft of the Model Rules of Professional Responsibility does not propose radical changes in the lawyer's adversary role. The Rules do not subject lawyers to any duties to which they are not already subject by virtue of existing positive law.

Janofsky, Leonard S. "The Future of the Legal Profession and the Role of the American Bar Association." The University of Toledo Law Review 11 (Winter 1980), 201-215.

Discusses aspects of social change to be expected over the next decade and the responses the legal profession intends to make. Janofsky notes the increase of attorneys in government service, corporate practice and more women practicing law. He indicates that there will be a need for legal training in non-advocacy aspects of law and recommends developing new and innovative means to deliver legal services.

Katz, Alan N. and Mark P. Denbeaux. "Trust, Cynicism and Machiavellianism Among Entering First Year Law Students." University of Detroit Journal of Urban Law 53 (1976), 397.

Analyzes interviews and other data gathered from law students to determine whether they conformed with the sterotype of attorneys as crafty and manipulative. The authors conclude that students trust people and respect professional ethics.

Kelso, Charles D. "Conflict, Emotion, and Legal Ethics." Pacific Law Journal 10:1 (Jan. 1979), 69-93.

The Code of Professional Responsibility can help resolve psychological and emotional conflicts at different stages in the lawyer-client relationship. A classification scheme explains how psychological and ethical dilemmas interrelate. It is based on the American Bar Association Code of Professional Responsibility and the psychological taxonomy of Andrew Watson, a law professor and psychiatrist. The scheme helps lawyers identify emotional conflicts that may exist and neutralize or resolve them by encouraging responsible professional conduct. Other conflicts discussed relate to the lawyer's need for recognition and self-aggrandizement; feelings of psychological responsibility for the client's moral status; and concerns about fees, competence, client rejection of advice and case outcome.

Kutak, Robert J. "Coming: The New Model Rules of Professional Conduct." American Bar Association Journal 66 (1980), 46-49.

Announces the publication of the discussion draft of the Model Rules of Professional Conduct. The Rules are founded in an analysis of the lawyer's function in various kinds of lawyer-client relationships rather than the lawyer's membership in the profession. The rules, though legislative and partly penal in character, recognize a measure of professional discretion regarding ethical choices among competing values.

Kutak, Robert J. "The Rules of Professional Conduct in An Era of Change." <u>Emory Law Journal</u> 29 (1980), 889-908.

Discusses the nature of changes that are currently affecting the function and responsibilities of the bar in American society and ways in which the Code of Professional Responsibility must be revised to accomodate those changes. Particular attention is focused on corporate and government practice.

Kutak, Robert J. "The Next Step in Legal Ethics -- Some Observations About the Proposed Model Rules of Professional Conduct." <u>Catholic University Law Review</u> 30:1 (1980), 1-12.

Considers two questions about the proposed Model Rules of Professional Conduct. First, why should the 1969 Code be replaced after so short a period of time? He answers that new rules are needed because the legal profession has changed rapidly. For example, very few attorneys still belong to independent private firms, and more legal services are being made available to low income people. Also, the old code is incomplete. For example, it does not consider various roles for lawyers, like corporate counsel, negotiator or advisor. Second, how do the proposed rules differ from the Code? Kutak says the old code is a "black letter statement" of the practice of ethical lawyering at the end of the 20th century, whereas the new rules treat the roles separately and recognize the dilemmas of ethical choice such as confidentiality.

Kutak, Robert J. "Proposed Model Rules of Professional Conduct." <u>Business Lawyer</u> 36 (1981), 573-584.

Describes the work of the ABA Commission on Evaluation of Professional Standards and the proposed Model Rules of Professional Conduct. Kutak describes the rules governing corporate practice, intra-firm ethical responsibilities, and limitations upon the attorney-client privilege.

Luban, David. "Professional Ethics - A New Code for Lawyers." Hastings Center Report 10:3 (June 1980), 11-15.

Criticizes the American Bar Association's Proposed Rules of Professional Conduct, arguing that the provisions requiring disclosure of information obtained from a client which affects the interests of third parties are ineffective. Luban contends the rules provide only illusory protection of affected third parties because they give the attorney too much discretion.

Lumbard, Thomas. "Setting Standards: The Courts, the Bar, and the Lawyers' Code of Conduct." Catholic University Law Review 30 (1981), 249-271.

Describes efforts of the American Bar Association and other organizations to revise or replace the Code of Professional Responsibility. Lumbard believes these efforts are ineffective and that a more appropriate method is for state courts to create an interstate body for formulating uniform standards of conduct. This alternative would be based on the courts' authority to regulate the practice of law.

Myers, Alan C. "The Attorney-Client Relationship and the Code of Professional Responsibility: Suggested Attorney Liabilty for Breach of Duty to Disclose Fraud to the Securities and Exchange Commission." Fordham Law Review 44 (May 1976), 1114-1144.

The imposition of increased obligations and liabilties on securities lawyers threatens not only the attorney, but the quality of his representations as well. Myers examines the possible consequences of the current expansion of liabilty and suggests what the securities lawyers' obligations and liabilities should be under DR 7-102 (B) (1) and DR 4-101 (C) (3) of the Code of Professional Responsibility.

Maru, Olavi. Annotated Code of Professional Responsibility. Chicago: American Bar Foundation, 1979.

The code is annotated with extensive notes and commentary analyzing court decisions and American Bar Association ethical opinions. The history of the Code, through successive drafts and subsequent amendments, is also recounted.

Patterson, L. Ray. "The Function of a Code of Legal Ethics." University of Miami Law Review 35 (1981), 695-726.

The lawyer-client relationship must be regarded as more than a mere agency-principal relationship because clients have duties and lawyers have rights. Rules of ethics should be integrated with positive law so that the rights and duties of both parties would be defined. This should be done by the bar itself before the courts intervene.

Patterson, L. Ray. "A Preliminary Rationalization of the Law of Legal Ethics." North Carolina Law Review 57 (1979), 519-558.

Argues that an effective code of professional ethics must correlate ethical and legal rules of conduct without confusing the two. Patterson criticizes the present Code for containing disciplinary rules that are derived from ethical principles and may, therefore, be avoided in an assertion of ethical ground.

Patterson, L. Ray. "Wanted: A New Code of Professional Responsibility." American Bar Association Journal 63 (1977), 639-642.

Argues that the time has come to abandon the hortatory ethical tone of the canons and to adopt rules of ethical conduct for the profession. Patterson criticizes the present code as rigid, simplistic, complex, contradictory and difficult to read. It does not provide the individual lawyer with adequate guidelines to deal with ethical problems because it does not reflect the realities of legal practice, especially the fact that different ethical problems arise in different sorts of legal practice.

Pickholz, Marvin G. "The Proposed Model Rules of Professional Conduct - And Other Assaults Upon the Attorney-Client Relationship: Does 'Serving the Public Interest' Disserve the Public Interest?" Business Lawyer 36 (July 1981), 1841-1862

A brief survey of historically accepted concepts of a lawyer's proper function. Pickholz discusses the reasons the proposed model rules and other efforts to limit attorney-client confidentiality in corporate practice interfere with the attorney's duty to serve the objective interests of his client.

Posner, Richard A. "The Ethical and Political Basis of the Efficiency Norm in Common Law Adjudication." <u>Hofstra Law Review</u> 8 (1979), 487-551.

Argues that a society that aims at maximizing wealth will produce an ethically attractive combination of happiness, rights, and sharing with less fortunate members of society. This is not true of a society that aims at maximizing happiness. Posner discusses how this wealth maximization aim is an attractive objective to guide common law adjudication and hence has played an important role in shaping substantive rules and procedures of the common law.

Report of the Joint Committee on Professional Responsibility. <u>American Bar Association Journal</u> 44 (1958), 1159, 1162, 1216-1218.

An attempt to set forth the rationale behind the Canons of Ethics in order to enable lawyers and law students to adhere more closely to the high standards of professionalism embodied in them.

Schnapper, Eric. "The Myth of Legal Ethics: The Moral Platitudes Found in the Code of Professional Responsibility Have Little to Do with Legal Ethics as Actually Enforced." <u>American Bar Association Journal</u> 64 (February 1978), 202-205.

Argues that the Code of Professional Responsibility is enforced only in cases involving theft of clients' funds, failure to provide services clients have paid for and attorney felony convictions. The less easily proven offenses against other provisions of the Code are rarely the subject of disciplinary proceedings for three reasons: the bar is self-regulating and hence self-serving; the sanctions available are too drastic; and clients are not likely to complain about attorney behavior if they win. The bar's failure to raise its ethical standards may result in greater constitutionalization of legal ethics and new constraints on the attorney-client privilege.

Sears, Dan W. "A Re-evaluation of the Canons of Professional Ethics - A Professor's Viewpoint." <u>Tennessee Law Review</u> 33 (1966), 145-161.

Argues that the Canons are severely deficient in providing clients with guidance on access to legal specialties. They are directed almost entirely to the litigation aspect of practice and are not useful in guiding attorneys in their other professional roles.

Selinger, Carl M. "The Perry Mason Perspective and Others: A Critique of Reductivist Thinking About the Ethics of Untruthful Practices by Lawyers for Innocent Defendants." Hofstra Law Review 6 (Spring 1978), 631-663.

Takes issue with a tendency among legal scholars to assume that what lawyers may ethically do can be deduced easily from what clients may ethically do, and that the rules for governing professional conduct may be derived from that mode of inquiry. Selinger discusses the ethics of untruthful conduct in criminal cases from the perspectives of innocent defendants, lawyers who believe their clients are innocent, and rule-makers for the legal profession.

Shaffer, Thomas L. "Christian Theories of Professional Responsibility." Southern California Law Review 48 (1975), 721-759.

Seeks to relate Christian values to those embodied in the Code of Professional Responsibility, which is inspired by positive secular impulses toward social utility. Mere social utility cannot provide the moral foundation for a truly Christian lawyer. Shaffer argues that a lawyer's commitment to helping people infuses the precepts of the Code with moral depth in practice.

Shuchman, Philip. "Ethics and Legal Ethics: The Propriety of the Canons as a Group Moral Code." George Washington Law Review 37 (1968), 244-269.

Examines those canons most frequently violated, noting that they concern obtaining clients and law as a business. These canons work to the disadvantage of small practitioners and are meant to codify the style of practice that only large law firms can afford to follow. Shuchman discusses their differential impact upon lower income groups who might be benefited through competitive legal practice.

Sonde, Theodore. "Continuing Debate on Attorney's Responsibilities to the Public and Third Parties." Business Lawyer 36 (1981), 585-589.

Discussion of the American Bar Association's proposed Model Rules of Professional Conduct. Sonde favors their division into categories representing various types of attorney functions with sets of rules appropriate to each. He describes how questionable practices in securities law practice led the SEC to require practitioners to consider the public interest. He sees this as an essential impetus to revise thinking on professional responsibility.

State Bar of California. Office of Professional Standards of the Division of Competence. California Compendium on Professional Responsibility. San Francisco, CA: The State Bar of California, 1983.

Includes a comprehensive index, The Rules of Professional Conduct of the State Bar of California, The State Bar Act, The American Bar Association Model Code of Professional Responsibility, and California ethics opinions. An annual subscription service is available.

Sutton, John F., Jr. "How Vulnerable is the Code of Professional Responsibility?" North Carolina Law Review 57 (1979), 497-517.

Argues that the Code of Professional Responsibility must be amended to minimize tensions between the needs of the client and those of third parties. Sutton discusses standards and formats for a revised code.

Sutton, John F., Jr. "Re-evaluation of the Canons of Professional Ethics: A Reviser's Point of View." Tennessee Law Review 33 (1966), 132-144.

Discusses the general characteristics desirable in a code of professional ethics. Such a code must appeal to reason yet serve as a basis for discipline; identify and explicate the principles basic to the function of the profession; provide authoritative standards; and be in harmony with commercial aspects of providing legal services.

Terapack, Richard G. "Administering Ethics Laws: The Ohio Experience." National Civic Review 68 (February 1979), 82-84.

Examines the impact of the 1973 ethics law in Ohio, noting that the general purpose of the legislation was to restore public confidence in the system. Ohio statistics indicate that candidates and public officials have not been driven away by financial disclosure.

Tischner, Paul A. "Lawyer Morality." George Washington Law Review 38 (1970), 789-848.

Argues that the legal profession must become concerned with morality. Adopting a code, though, would deny lawyers freedom of choice and serve merely to make them appear ethical. Code morality has been determined without reference to actual moral problems and isolates moral value from the circumstances of its application.

Tondel, Lyman M. "Watergate: The Public Lawyer and the Bar As Seen From the Perspective of the American Bar Association Ethics Committee." Business Lawyer 30 (1975), 295-298.

Tondel, chairman of the American Bar Association Ethics Committee, evaluates the charges levelled against Watergate defendants and considers whether amendments to the Code would have been effective in dealing with them. He argues that the standards of the profession, not the Code, should be raised so that lawyers may provide moral leadership.

Vernon, George. "The Illinois Code of Professional Responsibility: A Blueprint for Disciplinary Enforcement." DePaul Law Review 30 (1981), 365-401.

Highlights the fundamental themes of the recently adopted Code of Professional Responsibility in Illinois, including attorney-client confidences, solicitations, fees, clients' funds and conflicts of interest. Vernon details the applicability of the Code in limiting the activities of former government lawyers in private practice involving their former employer.

Wallace, James E. "The Code of Professional Responsibility - Legislated Irrelevance?" Texas Law Review 48 (1970), 311-333.

The Code of Professional Responsibility fails to give adequate ethical and disciplinary guidelines for the process of attorney specialization. Wallace warns that if the Code does not do so, specialists will seek guidance elsewhere.

Wright, Edward L. "The Code of Professional Responsibility: Its History and Objectives." Arkansas Law Review 24:1 (Spring 1970), 1-18.

Outlines the historical development of the Code, suggesting it treats the legal profession as an inherent part of the legal system. Ideal standards are set by the ethical considerations, while minimum standards are imposed by the disciplinary rules. The Code is compared with its predecessor, the Canons of Professional Ethics.

B. LAWYERS' ETHICS

American Bar Association. The Bar Foundation: Recognizing a Professional and Public Responsibility. Chicago: American Bar Association Press, 1979.

Handbook describing how to create a bar foundation. Such foundations are advanced as a response to the need to extend the availability of legal services; improve the administration of justice; strengthen efforts to promote high standards of professional performance, conduct, and legal education; and to counter public cynicism about the role of law and lawyers in American society.

American Bar Association. Consortium for Professional Education. Chicago: American Bar Foundation. Dilemmas in Legal Ethics (videotapes).

Five videocassettes deal with ethical issues faced by attorneys in their day-to-day practice. Problems arising in common and important lawyering tasks, such as interviewing, negotiation, investigation, counseling, and advocacy, are presented by casts of professional actors and lawyers. Following each dramatization, a group of panelists discusses the ethical issues and evaluates the conduct of the lawyers. The sixth videotape features discussion and debate on the subject of lawyer advertising, utilizing television "spots," model ads and excerpts from hearings and conferences conducted by the American Bar Foundation in 1975.

Archer, Gleason L. Ethical Obligations of the Lawyer. (Reprint of 1910 ed.) Littleton, CO: Rothman and Co., 1981.

Discusses the ethical duties of lawyers in public, professional and private situations. Archer contrasts the status of lawyers with laymen and discusses the nature of a lawyer's duties to his client (unswerving loyalty and an obligation not to overcharge), the adverse party, other lawyers, the courts and the state. He outlines the ethical obligations of lawyers in politics and business, and concludes with a description of their liability to clients and the conditions of disbarment and suspension.

Bedau, Hugo M. "Rough Justice...". Hastings Center Report (December 1978), 8-11.

Discusses the ethics of novel defenses. Television is alleged to have influenced battered spouses to commit murder or the police erroneously to kill a victim thought to be armed. The justification or excuse is presented to the jury as a species of mistake or insanity. Bedau considers the ethical aspect of attorneys' presenting such a defense.

Bloom, Murray Teigh. The Trouble With Lawyers. New York: Simon and Schuster, 1968.

Argues that the American middle class is victimized by the legal profession because, though it has money and property, it lacks group power in state legislatures. Hence, laws affecting the middle class needs tend to be drafted to maximize the role of legal counsel. Bloom cites examples in civil litigation, divorce, the sale of a home or business, and probate.

Carrington, Paul. "The Ethical Crises of American Lawyers." University of Pittsburgh Law Review 36 (1974), 35-54.

Surveys a perceived moral crisis in American society and warns that efforts to restore morality through legislation are mistaken. In the case of the legal profession, its members are better represented by the organized bar which has long been making progress toward the solution of the ethical crisis.

Cohen, Elliot D. "Two Concepts of a Lawyer." Unpublished monograph. Indian River Community College: Fort Pierce, FL. 24 pp.

Contrasts the model of a morally good person with two models of a good attorney; one functional and one "extreme." A functionally good attorney is the opposite of a morally good person. The extreme model, however, combines moral rectitude with professional excellence.

Cohen, Lucy Kramer, ed. _The Legal Conscience: Selected Papers of Felix S. Cohen._ New Haven: Yale University Press, 1960.

A collection of essays that discuss law, logic and ethics. Topics include the functional approaches to jurisprudence, law and language, judicial logic and the philosophical aspects of human rights. Contains sections on ethical and legal aspects of the law relating to the American Indians and the philosophy of American democracy.

Drinker, Henry S. _Legal Ethics_. New York: Columbia University Press, 1953.

A modern classic containing chapters on the history of the bar in England and the United States, the nature and history of the canons of professional ethics and disciplinary procedures in both countries.

Freedman, Monroe H. "Personal Responsibility in a Professional System." _Catholic University Law Review_ 27 (1975), 191-206.

The notion of role differentiation enables the professional to apply different moral standards in professional and personal capacities. This differentiation does not of necessity lead to professional amorality. The professional must put the moral choice to his client, not preempt his client's judgment: to do otherwise would amount to an assault on the client's autonomy.

Gerson, Allen, ed. _Lawyer's Ethics_. New Brunswick, NJ: Transaction Books, 1980.

A comprehensive and useful anthology representing critical thinking by lawyers about professional roles and responsibilities. Presents ethical dilemmas and balances competing considerations.

Glenn, Peter G. "Alternative Aproaches to Legal Ethics." Review of Ethics in the Practice of Law, by Geoffrey C. Hazard and Crisis At the Bar: Lawyers' Unethical Ethics and What To Do About It, by Jethro K. Lieberman. Texas Law Review 57 (1979), 307-320.

Discusses two approaches to the reform of legal ethics. Lieberman seeks revision of the Code of Professional Responsibility to reflect modern practices and values. Hazard argues that the Code should be discarded and a new ethos developed from a thorough analysis of the character of modern legal practice. Glenn is in agreement with Hazard.

Greenawalt, Kent. "Conflicts of Law and Morality - Institutions of Amelioration." Virginia Law Review 67 (1981), 177-236.

Discusses the criteria officials might use to decide which lawbreakers may justifiably be excused from punishment - specifically, the appropriate response of officials in the system of legal punishment to lawbreakers' claims that they acted out of compelling necessity or were within their moral rights. He explores the factors to be considered in such decisions, including the purposes of criminal law and the proper bases for social interference with individual freedom.

Greenebaum, Edwin H. "Attorneys' Problems in Making Ethical Decisions." Indiana Law Journal 52:1 (1979), 627-635.

Discusses legal ethics in light of emotional problems of decision-making, limitations on attorneys' freedom of choice, the position of the individual attorney as a member of a group, and the implications of client-oriented values. Greenebaum argues that attorneys, as advocates, should neither implicate themselves in wrongdoing nor confuse or obstruct the search for truth.

Halper, Thomas. "'Responsibility': An Effort at Clarification." Loyola University of Los Angeles Law Review 12 (1978), 7-35.

Discusses various aspects of the nature of responsibility: descriptive, judgmental, collective, relational, normative and determining. Halper concludes that both the external and internal means of determining responsibility are utilized in society, but that internal means for determining one's own responsibility, while more effective, are underutilized.

Hazard, Geoffrey C. "The Lawyer's Obligation to be Trustworthy When Dealing with Opposing Parties." South Carolina Law Review 33 (1981), 181-195.

Contends the Code cannot provide for lawyers' trustworthiness in dealing with opposing parties. Hazard argues that trustworthiness requires full material disclosure, but because opposing attorneys differ in technical sophistication, a rule requiring reciprocal sharing of information would not yield reciprocity.

Held, Virginia. "The Division of Moral Labor and the Role of the Lawyer." From The Good Lawyer ed. David Luban. Totowa, NJ: Rowman & Allanheld, 1984, pp. 60-79.

Asks whether lawyers have a morality which is different from and sometimes even in conflict with the morality of others. Held considers the lawyers' role from a point of view which asks what morally responsible lawyers are permitted to do and prohibited from doing, and what morally responsible lawyers can do to make the role and practices of law morally more justifiable.

Johnstine, Quintin and Dan Hopson, Jr. Lawyers and Their Work: An Analysis of the Legal Profession in the United States and England. Indianapolis, IN: Bobbs-Merrill, 1967.

Describes the services provided by lawyers in the United States and England and alternatives for providing those services. The authors' purpose is to identify areas where a more efficient means of providing legal services might be practicable.

Knight, Richard F. "Professional Responsibility." Louisiana Law Review 40 (Spring 1980), 728-741.

Discusses case law generated by the appellate courts of Louisiana in recent years dealing with questions of attorney's professional responsibility. Topics include prior convictions, commingling of clients' funds, advertising and solicitation, fees and malpractice.

Leventhal, Harold. "Professional Responsibility: Keynote Address of the Second Annual Baron De Hirsch Meyer

Lecture Series." *University of Miami Law Review* 30 (1976), 789-802.

Examines the concept of professional responsibility from various perspectives, discussing better ways to serve legal consumers through consideration of the duty to provide important counsel; the acceleration of the appellate process; an increase in judicial action; a re-examination of confidentiality and conflict of values between lawyer and client; and the need for lawyers to represent the public interest.

Lieberman, Jethro K. *Crisis at the Bar - Lawyers' Unethical Ethics and What to Do About It*. New York: W.W. Norton, 1978.

Contends that the ethical system of the American Bar is in disarray. This criticism covers the Code of Ethics; the failure of self-regulation; advertising and soliciting; fees; conflicts of interest of corporate and government attorneys; and attorneys' roles as counselors, negotiators and lobbyists.

Luban, David, ed. *The Good Lawyer: Lawyers' Roles and Lawyers' Ethics*. Totowa, NJ: Littlefield Adams, 1983.

Presents a variety of perspectives by philosophers, lawyers and legal scholars that probes assumptions in the legal profession. They examine such issues as problems of zeal, confidentiality, client perjury, psychic and moral costs of law practice and the morality of representing immoral causes. The book is designed as a theoretical and practical guide to basic issues confronting lawyers.

Luban, David. "Paternalism and the Legal Profession." *Wisconsin Law Review* 3 (1981), 453-493.

Discusses instances where substituting the attorney's judgment for the client's wishes may be justified, and illustrates with examples drawn from court cases.

Marks, F. Raymond. *The Lawyer, The Public and Professional Responsibility*. Chicago, IL: American Bar Foundation, 1972.

Examines the nature, causes, and viability of the private bar's responses to demands from the public and from young lawyers that the legal profession work more actively in serving the public interest. Explores the extent to which lawyers can serve both economic self-interest and public interest and remain professionals in the classic sense. Discusses what the profession must do to justify maintenance of its monopoly over the practice of law. Considers ways to distribute the economic burden of public interest work. Contains an appendix on methodology and an index.

Maru, Olavi. Bar Association Ethics Opinions. Chicago, IL: American Bar Foundation, 1985.

An addition to the earlier Supplement to the Digest of Bar Association Ethics Opinions which was published in 1982 and covered the period 1976-1980. This new supplement organizes, records, digests and indexes new materials as they are received on a continuing program basis.

McKay, Robert B. "Beyond Professional Responsibility." Capital University Law Review 10 (1981), 709-719.

Argues that the concept of professional responsibility must be broadened to apply to a view of the legal profession's function that is more than client-centered and litigation-focused. The profession should awaken to its responsibility to seek better ways to accomplish the ends of justice through an economical and efficient legal system.

Mellinkoff, David. The Conscience of a Lawyer. St. Paul, MN: West Publishing Co., 1977.

Uses the circumstances of a notorious 19th-century British murder trial to explore the ethical and moral problems of the attorneys involved. The fact that all evidence was circumstantial and that the police had botched their investigation made it an easy case for the defense. But the murderer confessed, thereby raising the question whether the defense should fully exploit the flaws in the prosecution case.

Petrowitz, Harold C. "Some Thoughts About Current Problems in Legal Ethics and Professional Responsibility." Duke Law Journal 1979:6 (1979), 1275-1290.

Discusses the ABA's responses to ethical problems facing attorneys in specified practice. These include knowledge that a client or another attorney is engaged in unlawful activity, and an attorneys' leaving government service to join law firms that deal with their former employers. Petrowitz criticizes relevant provisions of the Code of Professional Responsibility.

Pike, James A. Beyond the Law: The Religious and Ethical Meaning of the Lawyers' Vocation. New York: Doubleday and Co., 1963.

Argues that society, religion and the legal profession hold a total claim upon attorneys to exercise a high degree of professional responsibility. Also, the lawyer has a need to view himself as a professional of impeccable integrity.

Postema, Gerald J. "Moral Responsibility in Professional Ethics." New York University Law Review 55:1 (April 1980), 63-89.

Argues for a new conception of professional ethics in which lawyers must acknowledge personal responsibility for their professional conduct. Postema suggests that a new code of professional responsibility is required because the current code allows lawyers to ignore the social and moral costs of their actions and to do as professionals what they would not do as individuals.

Postema, Gerald. "Self-Image, Integrity, and Professional Responsibility." From The Good Lawyer ed. David Luban. Totowa, NJ: Rowman & Allanheld, 1984, pp. 286-314.

Useful philosophical contributions to the debate over professional ethics are made when philosophers who take professional situations and problems seriously call attention to and critically assess the ways professionals approach and deal with moral problems. Postema focuses on existing conceptions of professional roles and on particular conceptions of the lawyers role. He concludes we should spend less time trying to define the content and limits of professional responsibility and more time trying to understand the social and institutional conditions of morally responsible professional behavior.

Pound, Roscoe. "What Is a Profession? The Rise of the Legal Profession in Antiquity." Notre Dame Lawyer 19 (1944), 203-228.

Treats a profession as a learned art pursued more as a public service than a livelihood. Pound discusses the varied professional functions of the attorney including his roles a advisor, agent, teacher and advocate. He traces the development of the attorney's role from Helenic society to the present.

Roberts, Denys. How to Dispense With Lawyers. London: Frederick Muller, 1964.

The bar and the courts are lampooned in the English manner. Ten chapters include: Courts of Law; The System and the Civil Courts; Criminal and Other Courts; Judges; Lawyers; The Civil Litigant out of Court; Selecting Your Bench and Jury; The Litigant in Court; Advocacy; and Evidence.

Rodell, Fred. Woe Unto You, Lawyers. 2nd ed. New York: Pageant Press, 1957.

Criticizes the law and the legal system. Rodell exposes defects in the legal system and proposes greater efforts to codify existing law to limit the influence of lawyers and judges who, he feels, are motivated largely by selfishness.

Rostow, Eugene V. The Ideal in Law. Chicago: University of Chicago Press, 1978.

A collection of Rostows' writings on the relationship between law and ethics and the nature and function of law. Laws and customs resulting in discrimination against negroes provide a basis for an ethical criticism of law as an embodiment of custom. Rostow discusses civil disobedience and its limits, and the scope of the lawyer-client privilege to illustrate another kind of conflict between ethics and law. He also discusses ethical problems of official economic policy and international relations.

Rutherglen, George. "Conflicts of Law and Morality - The Relevance of Legal Reasoning." Virginia Law Review 67 (1981), 237-248.

Argues that a lawbreaker's sincere moral conviction that his deviant act is justified should not be a relevant factor in ameliorating the mechanical operation of law. Such emphasis on state of mind diverts attention from the moral argument itself. Rutherglen argues that it is improper to base decisions on the conformity of the lawbreaker's moral justification to prevailing moral opinion.

Schwartz, Murray L. "Professionalism and Accountability of Lawyers." California Law Review 66:4 (1978), 669-697.

Focuses on the principles which should apply to the lawyer in a non-adversarial setting, proposing a professional rule that would restrain such lawyers from using unconscionable means or working for unconscionable ends. Schwartz argues that non-advocates cannot claim immunity from moral accountability accorded advocates.

Shaffer, Thomas L. On Being a Christian and a Lawyer: Law for the Innocent. Provo, Utah: Brigham Young University Press, 1980.

Discusses the ethics of the lawyer's role in client counseling with an emphasis on representing the guilty client. Advocacy is seen as a process of reconciliation and a moral discourse before the community. Shaffer discusses the moral responsibilities of law students and faculties.

Shaffer, Thomas L. "The Practice of Law as Moral Discourse." Notre Dame Lawyer 55 (1979), 231-253.

Identifies three ethical orientations in the practice of law. According to role orientation the lawyer's function in society provides the ethical parameters. On the second, moral isolation, the relationship between the attorney and his client provides its own moral parameters: the lawyer's duty is to apprise his client of choices and respect the client's decision, while permitting the attorney to withdraw on questions of conscience. Shaffer advocates a third orientation - to care for the client and to be cared for by him - but notes an imbalance between power and concern.

Stephens, William T. "The Alabama Ethics Cases." Cumberland - Samford Law Review 10 (1979), 317-357.

Describes lawsuits arising under the Alabama ethics law which prohibits persons in positions of public trust from using their positions for personal gain. The law has stringent financial disclosure provisions and the state Ethics Commission has wide investigatory powers to examine the affairs of public officials.

Stern, Duke N. Review of Crisis at the Bar: Lawyers' Unethical Ethics and What to Do About It, by Jethro Lieberman. American Bar Association Journal 64 (Sept. 1978), 1403-1404.

Credits Lieberman's style with provoking reflection on the ethics that are the underpinnings of the legal profession. Lieberman argues that lawyers are despised because they persist in relying on an unethical code of ethics. Questionable aspects of modern practice are attacked and self-regulation of the bar is described as inadequate. Lieberman proposes more public control of the professions, wider representation in bar policy-making bodies, less stringent limits on who may practice law, and law enforcement agencies involvement in regulation of practice violations. The reviewer found the book biased, but well-researched and provocative.

Stern, Philip M. Lawyers on Trial. New York: New York Times Books, 1980.

Explores the "dark side" of the legal profession. Stern finds legal education prepares law students to serve the interests of the profession and the affluent. He criticizes the bar's monopoly and obstructionism in reporting services and its consistent stance against progressive legislation such as no-fault divorce and legal insurance. He alleges that the bar uses admission requirements to screen out individuals who would upset the profession's status quo.

Stewart, Potter. "Professional Ethics for the Business Lawyer: The Morals of the Market Place." Business Lawyer 31:1 (1975), 463-468.

Discusses Goldfarb v. Virginia State Bar in which the petitioners brought a class action suit against the county and state bar associations claiming that the minimum fee schedule for legal services constitutes price-fixing, a violation of the Sherman Act. The U.S. Supreme Court held that it indeed was a violation. Justice Stewart believes that the public is best served in a competitive legal marketplace. He adheres to the proposition that the ethics of the business lawyer are -- and perhaps should be -- no more than the morals of the marketplace.

Sturm, Douglas. "American Legal Realism and the Covenantal Myth: World Views in the Practice of Law.: Mercer Law Review 31 (1980), 487-508.

Utilizes the myth of the covenant to illustrate how the practice of law might come to be seen by practitioners as a means to liberate the oppressed, do justice and tend to the needs of the community as opposed to the utilitarian view of law embodied in current practice.

Trumbull, William M. Materials on the Lawyer's Professional Responsibility. Englewood Cliffs, NJ: Prentice-Hall, 1957.

A collection on legal ethics, admission to the bar, professional discipline and the organization of the bar. Topics include judiciary relationships with clients and others; the attorney-client privilege; criminal practice; professional fees; solicitation and advertising; and relations with other lawyers, clients and the public.

Wallingford, Whitney. "Professional Responsibility." Kentucky Law Journal 67 (1978-1979), 757-774.

Discusses the interpretations given U.S. Supreme Court decisions dealing with various aspects of professional responsibility and qualifications by the appellate courts of Kentucky. The cases discussed involve advertising, solicitation, and professional and extra-professional misconduct.

Warvelle, George W. Essays in Legal Ethics, 2nd ed. Chicago: Callaghan & Co., 1920.

This compendium of lectures on legal ethics given by Warvelle as a teacher of law covers the nature of ethics; moral and ethics distinguished; the nature of advocacy; the lawyer's function as an officer of the court; advertising and solicitation; fees; general and criminal practice; and relations with courts, clients and the bar.

Wasserstrom, Richard. "Lawyers as Professionals: Some Moral Issues." Human Rights 5 (Fall 1975), 1-24.

Examines two moral criticisms of the lawyer-client relationship. First, it renders the lawyer at best amoral, and at worst immoral in dealing with the rest of the world. Second, the lawyer inevitably treats the client in an impersonal, paternalistic, and domineering fashion.

Wolf, Susan. "Ethics, Legal Ethics, and the Ethics of Law." From The Good Lawyer ed. David Luban. Totowa, NJ: Rowman & Allanheld, 1984, pp. 38-59.

Offers a different conception of the subject of legal ethics that substantially concedes the point of those who object to the practice of law. Yet Wolf does not admit that no consideration of ethical principles and virtues has special relevance or special force to the members of the legal profession.

Zemans, Frances K. and Victor G. Rosenblum. The Making of a Public Profession. Chicago, IL: American Bar Foundation, 1981.

Reports on a study of law school education and its impact on professionalization of lawyers, providing an empirically based assessment of lawyers' perspectives on legal education. The book is divided into eight chapters, among them: Designing Research on the professional Development of Lawyers; Route to the Legal Profession; Portrait of an Urban Bar; Credentials for Professional Status; Preparation for the Practice of Law; and Socialization to Professional Responsibility. Appendices include the questionnaire and a note on law school ratings. A twelve page bibliography is included.

CHAPTER TWO
LAW SCHOOL MATERIALS

A. LAW SCHOOL TEXTS

Aronson, Robert, and Donald Weckstein. Aronson and Weckstein's Professional Responsibility in a Nutshell. St. Paul, MN: West Publishing Co., 1980.

Outlines the law of professional responsibility. Designed as a study aid for law students.

Aronson, Robert H. Problems in Professional Responsibility. St. Paul, MN: West Publishing Co., 1978.

Contains problems and resources on professional responsibility. The problems presented are adapted from actual cases.

Auerbach, Jerold S. Unequal Justice: Lawyers and Social Change in Modern America. New York: Oxford University Press, 1976.

Examines the historical role of the American legal profession in social change. Contains a bibliographical essay describing sources Auerbach found useful, listing historical, biographical and sociological works. Author found no comprehensive work chronicling the history of the American bar had been written.

Bloom, Murray Teigh, ed. Lawyers, Clients and Ethics. New York: Council on Legal Education for Professional Responsibility, Inc., 1979.

Cases and materials discussing problems of professional responsibility. The issues discussed include perjured clients; fees; indigent and minority clients; and the use of questionable tactics for a client's interests.

Bonsignore, J. J., E. Katsh, P. D'Enrico, R. M. Pipkin, S. Arons, and J. Rifkin. Before the Law -- An Introduction to the Legal Process. 2nd ed. Boston, MA: Houghton Mifflin Co., 1979.

Outlines the major explanations of the nature of law as rules, values, competing interests, popular sentiments, power, and discretion. The book discusses judicial cases; perspectives on the police; lawyers' training and background; lawyers' role in social reform; the jury system; and corrections. The final section examines the development of law in interaction with legal and social forces. It is designed as a text, and each chapter is followed by questions and suggestions for additional reading.

Costigan, George P. Jr. Cases and Other Authorities on Legal Ethics. St. Paul, MN: West Publishing Co., 1917.

An early case book on legal ethics. Topics covered include the attorney-client relationship, advertising and solicitation, conflict of interest, the organization and purpose of bar associations, and the nature of the attorney's duty as an officer of the court.

Countryman, Vern. Problems of Professional Responsibility Under the Uniform Commercial Code. Philadelphia, PA: American Law Institute, 1969.

Presents professional responsibility problems likely to arise as a practitioner advises his client, negotiates on his behalf, or represents him in court under the rules of the Uniform Commercial Code. Materials are designed for legal education.

Dvorkin, Elizabeth, Jack Himmelstein, and Howard Lesnick. Becoming a Lawyer: A Humanistic Perspective on Legal Education and Professionalism. St. Paul, MN: West Publishing Co., 1981.

A collection of readings and commentary on such issues as identity within a professional role, personal awareness in professional development and self-expression through serving society.

Frank, Jerome. Law and the Modern Mind. New York: Tudor Publishing Company, 1936.

Applies psychological concepts to law and legal thought. Frank argues the acknowledgment of psychological process in legal thinking illuminates the interplay among ingrained attitudes, the psychological content of language, and the limits of formal logic in solving legal problems.

Hart, H. L. A. The Concept of Law. Oxford: Clarendon Press, 1961.

Analyzes the nature of law, coercion and morality, arguing that they are different but related. Hart describes the legal foundation of the relation between sovereign and subject. He discusses the foundations of the legal system and the differences and similarities between justice and morality, and law and morality.

Hazard, Geoffrey. Ethics in the Practice of Law. New Haven, CT: Yale University Press, 1980.

Analyzes the legal profession's crisis of public confidence and self-confidence. Hazard identifies three problems. First, serious questions remain about what the ethical rules are. Second, a lawyer's professional function consists of counseling clients about how to evade or mitigate legal obligations. Third, a tension exists between the client's particular professional position and the demand for equality that everyone is accorded by general principles of morality and legality. The book consists of eleven chapters which cover conflict of interest, unpopular clients, the adversary system, and advice and consent.

Kaufman, Andrew. Problems in Professional Responsibility. Boston, MA: Little, Brown & Co., 1976.

Casebook divided into 13 sections, including conflict of interest; confidentiality; lawyers' responsibility; special office and court issues; lawyers' special obligations to the court, the profession and society; access to legal services; admission to the bar; and discipline. Appendices include the Code of Professional Responsibility and the Code of Judicial Conduct. Tables of cases, citations and secondary authorities are also included.

Morgan, Thomas D. "Evolving Concept of Professional Responsibility." From Teaching Professional Responsibility -- Materials and Proceedings from the National Conference, by Patrick A. Keenan et al. Detroit, MI: University of Detroit School of Law, 1979, pp. 742-743.

Advocates reform of the American Bar Association's Code of Professional Responsibility in order to protect the interests of the public and the client. The Code is repeatedly biased in its ordering of priorities, and creates a self-serving ethic. An analysis of the Code indicates that the interest of the individual attorney is primary and the client's and public's concerns inferior. Restructuring the priorities of the Code is urged in order to develop programs of prepaid legal services and lawyer referral agencies.

Patterson, L. Ray. Legal Ethics: The Law of Professional Responsibility. New York: Bender, 1982.

This casebook is based on the premise that rules of conduct for lawyers are in fact rules of law rather than rules of ethics.

Pirsig, Maynard E. and Kenneth F. Kirwin. Cases and Materials on Professional Responsibility. 3rd ed. St. Paul, MN: West Publishing Co., 1976.

Covers the basis of professional responsibility, restricting the practice of law, availability of legal services, the nature and duties of the attorney-client relationship, limits upon advocacy and conflict of interest. Supplemented annually.

Pound, Roscoe. "Mechanical Jurisprudence." Columbia Law Review 8 (1908), 605-623.

Classic piece which identifies two dangers in a scientific (mechanical) legal system: First, the law may no longer be perceived by the public as animated by notions of fair play and justice; and second, the courts and the legal profession may be prevented from exercising independent consideration of new problems, leading to stagnation and dogmatism. The law may utilize scientific concepts and logical reasoning, but these should not be permitted to preclude a socially desirable result.

Redlich, Norman. Professional Responsibility: A Problem Approach. Boston, MA: Little, Brown and Co., 1976.

Contains materials on the nature of the lawyer-client relationship, the role of the lawyer as advocate, conflicts of interest, the special problems of government lawyers, and ethical tests.

Schwartz, Murray L. Lawyers and the Legal Profession: Cases and Materials. Indianapolis: Bobbs-Merrill, 1979.

This casebook is organized around two themes. Part I centers around the lawyer as a client's representative, moving from the lawyer's legal, professional and ethical problems within the adversary system to negotiating and counselling. It concludes with the conflicting obligations that lawyers face. Part II concerns the distribution of legal services, including geographical restrictions on the practice of law as well as intraprofessional restraints, like solicitation and advertising. Schwartz offers projections on the public interest movement. Finally, he examines legal services to the poor. Each chapter includes extensive case notes and questions for class discussion.

B. LEGAL EDUCATION

American Bar Association. "How Well Do Law Schools Teach Professional Responsibility?" Law Schools and Professional Education: Report and Recommendations of the Special Committee for a Study of Legal Education of the American Bar Association. Chicago, IL: American Bar Association Press, 1980, 55-62.

Summarizes the findings of two studies: Pipkin's analysis of law school instruction in professional responsibility and Zemans' and Rosenblum's study of Chicago lawyers. The ABA report recommends teaching professional responsibility at the undergraduate level because courses would not then be subject to a "pecking order" and the "cross pollination" of disciplines might heighten prospective lawyer's awareness of the ways others view the legal profession.

"Applied Ethics: A Strategy for Fostering Professional Responsibility." Carnegie Quarterly 28 (Spring/Summer 1980), 1-7.

The Hastings Center is playing a key role in the development of applied and professional ethics. Historically, ethics occupied an important place in education, but by the 20th century science displaced philosophical reasoning. However, ethics is recently emerging in a new form. Rather than studying the traditional theoretical approach, students are learning to apply ethical theory to fact through case studies.

Aronson, Robert H. "New Dimensions in Legal Ethics." Learning and the Law 2:3 (Fall 1975), 50-64.

Criticizes the Socratic method of teaching professional responsibility because it involves only a few students, and the lecture method because it involves no students. Aronson recommends clinical experience in which both students and teachers actively participate through role-playing.

Arthurs, Harry W. and Brian D. Bucknall. Bibliographies on the Legal Profession and Legal Education in Canada. Toronto, Ontario: York University, 1968.

Includes references on history, government, organization, sociology, methods of practice, compensation, ethics and professional conduct. Legal education items intion of law schools, characteristics of students and teachers, legal research, and specific law courses and post-graduate study.

Bell, Derrick A. "Black Students in White Law Schools: The Ordeal and the Opportunity." University of Toledo Law Review 1970 (1970), 539-558.

Considers the early development of legal education for black students. Bell examines the types of black students currently admitted to law school, concluding that their psychological and sociological experience makes the study of law very difficult for them. He criticizes law schools' failure to provide proper instructional and administrative assistance to help assure success.

Bellow, Gary, and Bea Moulton. The Lawyering Process: Materials for Clinical Instruction in Advocacy. Mineola, NY: The Foundation Press, 1978.

Contains three main kinds of materials. The first and third explore ways to learn a professional role and whether the values and attitudes are justifiable. The second examines these questions in the context of particular tasks and relationships, attempting to develop a critical perspective and common understanding about what the "law job" actually involves. The authors suggests two models, one sixty-hours and the other thirty-hours, for use in making lawyering a subject of inquiry.

Bond, Jesse H. "Present Instruction in Professional Ethics in Law Schools." American Law School Review 4 (1915), 40-45.

Compares time and money spent and methods used to teach legal ethics at 81 law schools and finds that most schools paid minimal attention to the subject, usually offering just a few lectures. Bond concludes that there is a movement toward increased curricular emphasis on legal ethics.

Bradner, James H., Jr. "Developing Law of Professional Responsibility." From Teaching Professional Responsibility -- Materials and Proceedings from the National Conference by Patrick A. Keenan et al. Detroit, MI: University of Detroit School of Law, 1979, pp. 923-936.

The public demands for a moderation of zealous advocacy and the protection of clients as consumers of legal services is a new role for lawyers. The practice of law is no longer left solely to the bar and the courts. Now clients expect to participate in the legal process. Increasingly, nonlawyers are becoming members of disciplinary boards. Bradner believes professional responsibility must go beyond the law school curriculum and become a part of peer review and continuing education.

Bresnahan, James F. "Ethics and the Study and Practice of Law: The Problem of Being Fuller in a Professional Sense." Journal of Legal Education 28 (1976), 184-209.

Notes a tension between the practicing bar and the teaching bar over how best to inculcate ethical sensitivity in law students. Mere inclusion of legal ethics courses in the law school curriculum is insufficient. Bresnahan suggests that a profitable comparison may be made with the experiences of the medical profession and recommends collaboration between a teaching bar and ethicists.

Bresnahan, James F. and John L. Kane. "Professional Ethics and Competence in Trial Practice." American Bar Association Journal 62 (August 1976), 998-991.

Describes ethics in the practice of law as a problem of uncertainty to be resolved through conceptual clarity. The authors believe that ethics in law must be a two-way consultation between lawyers as practitioners and ethicists as theorists. The concept of a "profession" should be taught as a dialogue between an attorney and an ethicist.

Burger, Warren E. "The Role of the Law School in the Teaching of Legal Ethics and Professional Responsibility." Cleveland State Law Review 29 (1980), 377-395.

Discusses the duty of the law school to inculcate principles of professional ethics and standards in its students. Burger emphasizes that the entire educational system must deal with these issues. Token courses on professional responsibility offered at law schools will not suffice. Law schools, bar associations and the bench must cooperate to achieve higher standards.

Burger, Warren E. "Some Further Reflections On the Problem of Adequacy of Trial Counsel." Fordham Law Review 39:1 (October 1980), 1-25.

Criticisms by the Chief Justice that law schools are not adequately preparing students to function as courtroom advocates. Burger urges a new emphasis on legal training in the development of trial advocacy skills.

Cheatham, Elliott E. "What the Law Schools Can Do to Raise the Standards of the Legal Profession." American Law Society Review 7 (1932), 716-735.

Discusses three ways to raise the standards of the legal profession. First, law schools may employ the "genteel tradition" by encouraging students to develop standards, emphasizing the honor system and citing biographies of great lawyers. Second, they may teach the code of professional conduct. Third, they can encourage the study of law as a professiona and as an aspect of social organization. Cheatham also discusses the role of bar associations and suggests ways for them to cooperate with law schools to raise standards.

Christenson, Gordon A. "Studying Law as the Possibility of Principled Action." Denver Law Journal 50 (1974), 413-437.

Discusses law schools' responsibility to prepare students for worldly success and for principled action. The latter requires a search for intellectual strength in a world of values and introspection. Christenson discusses the roles of clinical training in intellectual development. He regards the development of analytical and critical skills, creativity, artistry, restraint and systematic comprehension as an integral part of a good legal education.

Churchill, Larry R. "The Teaching of Ethics and Moral Values in Teaching: Some Contemporary Confusions." Journal of Higher Education 53 (1982), 296-306.

Discusses contemporary theories about whether moral values can be transmitted through ethics courses in a professional education setting. Churchill considers the nature of moral values, assumptions about how they are learned and the nature of the transmission of moral values in the teaching process. He believes that moral values permeate the educational process, but that often just what values are intrinsic to that process is not understood.

Clinical Education for the Law Student. The Council on Legal Education for Professional Responsibility. New York: Meilen Press, 1973.

Discusses clinical education as a method, education versus service, the delivery of legal services and other improvements in the machinery of justice, professional responsibility, the courtroom as a classroom, and clinical education and the law school budget.

Condlin, Robert. The Moral Failure of Clinical Legal Education. College Park, MD: Center for Philosophy and Public Policy, University of Maryland, 1981.

A critical evaluation of professional ethics in clinical legal education. Condlin criticizes the teacher-student relationship in a clinical setting as developing a shallow and self-serving sense of moral responsibility; manipulative interpersonal strategies in students who are effective in achieving professional success; and weakening their disposition to seek and speak truth. He feels that clinical legal education is not well enough understood by those who employ it and substantial study is still needed before it may achieve its potential.

Costigan, George P. Jr. "The Teaching of Legal Ethics." American Law Society Review 4 (1917), 290-296.

Describes the adoption of a legal ethics course at Northwestern University Law School in 1909 and students' attitudes toward it.

Elkins, James R. "Moral Discourse and Legalism in Legal Education." Journal of Legal Education 32 (1982), 11-52.

Contends legal education in professional responsibility as currently taught is ineffective because it is grounded in the practical problems of lawyering and is not informed by any theory of professional responsibility. It thus lacks depth and misleads students into separating the idea of moral conduct from ethical professional practice.

Elson, Alex. "Canon 2 - Bright and Dark Face of the Legal Profession." Teaching Professional Responsibility -- Materials and Proceedings from the National Conference, ed. Patrick A. Keenan. Detroit, MI: University of Detroit School of Law, 1979, pp. 951-980.

Discusses the monopoly of the legal profession over legal services, drawing attention to the people who cannot afford legal services yet need them. Background information is provided on the development and approval of legal assistance programs.

Fuller, Lon L. "What the Law Schools Can Contribute to the Making of Lawyers." Journal of Legal Education 1 (1948), 189-204.

Sets out four competing conceptions of the objectives of legal education in 1948. First, it can give the students knowledge, not merely inculcate methods but provide a framework within which the content becomes relevant. Second, it can impart skills, not as an exclusive standard of education, but as a by-product of the system. Third, it can expose the student to ideas of "great minds" on various facets of the profession. Fourth, it can develop an understanding of the adjudicative and legislative processes of the system.

Hellman, Lawrence K. "Considering the Future of Legal Education: Law Schools and Social Justice." Journal of Legal Education 29:64 (1978), 170-193.

Discusses the prospective role of law schools in fostering the wider distribution of legal services and high standards of personal morality in their graduates. Hellman suggests law schools may instill a sense of commitment to the highest moral standards and to social activism by emphasizing the search for fair results in cases discussed in classes and by the personal example of law faculty.

Katz, Michael. "Black Law Students in White Law Schools -- Law in a Changing Society." University of Toledo Law Review 1970: 2:3 (Spring/Summer 1970), 589-606.

Contends that blacks have been denied access to the process of formulating society's legal principles. The legal system has either treated blacks as a separate group subject to its own laws, such as slave codes or Jim Crow legislation, or it has considered blacks as a group not fully entitled to the protection of laws applicable to the rest of society. Although the U.S. Supreme Court has undone much of the damage wrought by its predecessors and most of the formal discriminations against blacks have been repealed, the situation of the black community in its structural relations with societal institutions has not changed at all. For blacks, the law, especially the police, has imposed violence and repression. What is needed is a reexamination of the legal system which will create a just and humane society. Black law students in white schools can play a major role in this effort.

Keenan, Patrick A., Ed. Teaching Professional Responsibility -- Materials and Proceedings from the National Conference. Detroit, MI: University of Detroit School of Law, 1979.

The proceedings and contributed materials from the National Conference on Teaching Professional Responsibility present varying perspectives on lawyers' ethical conduct. Argues that a course in professional responsibility must be required by every law school, and continuing education programs must include materials which maintain the sensitivity of the bar to issue professional ethics. Topics of conference presentations include innovations in the teaching of professional responsibility, student perceptions of attorneys' ethics, the scrutinizing of legal education, and moral conflicts in the legal profession. Specific papers discuss the teaching of required courses in professional ethics, the psychological perspective of legal education, and the moral foundations of the attorney-client relationship.

Kelly, Michael. Legal Ethics and Legal Education. Hastings-on-Hudson, NY: The Hastings Center, 1980.

Considers the functions and problems in the legal ethics course in terms of the development of legal education. Section II presents legal education in an historical context. Section III comments on current legal ethics teaching. Section IV reviews the kinds of materials commonly covered in courses and their goals. Section V proposes several suggestions to improve teaching. Kelly concludes that professional ethics cannot be separated from the institutional roles and mission of legal education.

Kelly, Michael. "Notes on the Teaching of Ethics in Law School." Journal of the Legal Profession 5 (1980), 21-29.

Argues that law school ethics courses do not ultimately provide students with the practical guidance necessary to make correct ethical decisions when faced with clients who seek legal assistance to achieve unlawful or socially harmful ends. Kelly recommends emphasizing clinical legal eduction and making the discussion of ethical considerations a pervasive topic throughout the curriculum.

Kelso, Charles D. "The Duty to Deliver Competent Counsel." University of Miami Law Review 30 (1976), 847-878.

Presents a statistical analysis of the procedures involved in the selection, function and training of lawyers. Kelso surveys law school curricula, the use of clinical programs and proposals to require practice-oriented courses as a prerequisite for admission to the bar. He criticizes the current system and argues that less emphasis should be placed on LSAT scores and that the multi-state bar examination should be given after the second year of law school.

Kinnane, Charles H. "Compulsory Study of Professional Ethics by Law Students." American Bar Association Journal 16 (1930), 222-224.

The American Bar Association first favored making Professional Ethics part of law school curriculum in 1929. This article outlines the reasons for this decision and argues that good moral character - as opposed to morality - will not always safely guide an attorney in cases involving professional decorum and in problematic cases arising out of the nature of the adversary system.

Lasswell, Harold D. and Myres S. McDougal. "Legal Education and Public Policy: Professional Training in the Public Interest." Yale Law Journal 52 (1943), 203-295.

Legal education can serve the needs of a free and productive commonwealth through conscious, efficient and systematic training for social policymaking. It must train lawyers to capitalize on their role as legal advisors to various policy makers in society and government.

Luban, David. Ethics and the Legal Profession: A Model Course. College Park MD: Center for Philosophy and Public Policy, University of Maryland, 1982.

Pamphlet containing the outline for a 15-week course in ethics and the legal profession.

The user is referred to materials such as philosophical works, law review articles, books and cases. Luban attempts to test and criticize the standard conception of a lawyer's duty - that he is obligated to help clients prevail regardless of the morality of the client's ends. This concept is examined in the context of the lawyer-client relationship and the legal and moral limitations that circumscribe it. The lawyer's obligations to himself, to third parties and to society are raised to challenge the standard concept. The pamphlet contains a syllabus and a summary of the issues to be covered during each week of the course.

Luban, David. "Calming the Hearse Horse: A Philosophical Research Program for Legal Ethics." Maryland Law Review 40 (1981), 451-476.

Argues that an adequate curriculum must not only examine specific provisions in the Code, but address general philosophical issues. Luban recommends that philosophical literature be developed on the conflicts between ordinary morality and role morality. He suggests two approaches: employ legal clinics that place students in a practical situation; and emphasize ethical analysis through course work.

McKay, Robert. "Ethical Standards for Law Teachers." Arkansas Law Review 25:44 (1971), 44-66.

Law teachers should regard themselves as bound by the Code of Professional Responsibility to provide sound ethical education as well as high standards of scholarly honesty.

Meltsner, Michael and Philip G. Schrag. "Scenes From a Clinic." University of Pennsylvania Law Review 127 (1978), 1-55.

The authors are directors of a clinical legal education project at Columbia University. They describe a law school clinic in which students are able to examine their goals, ethical obligations, a variety of learning techniques that may be useful to them in practice and the personal and group relationships they encounter as professionals.

Pipkin, Ronald M. "Law School Instruction in Professional Responsibility: A Curricular Paradox." American Bar Foundation Research Journal 2 (1979), 247-275.

Discusses the results of a study on law school instruction in professional responsibility (1975-76) conducted by the American Bar Foundation. Data were taken from a sample of law students to examine the influence of prevailing learning norms in legal education upon student responses to courses in professional responsibility. Pipkin reviews the basis of ambiguous sentiments about the role of education in professional ethics and concludes with a discussion of the difficulties and dilemmas involved in attempts to alter the established mode of instruction.

Pirsig, Maynard E. "Legal Profession." University of Colorado Law Review 41 (1969), 373-392.

Describes law school courses in legal ethics and outlines the topics that might be covered in a two hour course. Pirsig discusses the general trend of class discussion on such topics as specialization, unauthorized practice and the nature of a profession. He argues that such courses are important, but should be taught in conjunction with a more pervasive concern for issues in legal ethics to balance the law curriculum.

Redlich, Norman. "The Moral Value of Clinical Legal Education: A Reply to Professor Condlin." From The

Good Lawyer ed. David Luban. Totowa, NJ: Rowman & Allanheld, 1984, pp. 350-358.

Addresses a defense of clinical legal education that, if it can be sustained, not only supports clinical programs, especially those that take the form of live client relationships rather than simulation. Redlich argues, against Condlin, that clinical education provides an opportunity for the student to develop as a moral person and for the sound values of the legal profession to be infused into the process of legal education.

Savoy, Paul N. "Toward a New Politics of Legal Education." Yale Law Journal 79 (1970), 444-504.

Discusses dissatisfaction with the utilitarian propensities of legal education by students seeking greater personal satisfaction in a legal career through social activism. Savoy argues that there is a place for social activism and creativity in legal education and that a change in traditional pedagogical methods, such as abandoning grades and other structural aspects of legal education, might be a part of this improvement.

Schwartz, Murray. "Moral Development, Ethics and the Professional Education of Lawyers." Moral Development: Proceedings of the 1974 Educational Testing Service Invitational Conference pp. 32-41.

Contends law schools are poorly equipped to inculcate values in students. Students are already quite mature with established beliefs; faculties are small and university life does not encourage them to interact significantly with students; and the curriculum is more concerned with analysis and theory than with the ethical aspects of legal practice. The Code of Professional Responsibility also provides little guidance since it offers the attorney the choice of identifying totally with his client's interests or of withdrawing his services if his moral sensibilities are offended by his client's claim. In the former case the lawyer sets his own moral scruples aside; and in the latter the client can simply hire another attorney.

Shaffer, Thomas L. and Robert S. Redmount. Lawyers, Law Students and People. New York: McGraw-Hill, 1977.

Discusses legal education and the attitudes it imbues in those who undertake it. The authors describe the course of studies and pedagogical methods used in law schools. They recount the results of surveys of law students' attitudes, personal and social backgrounds, skills and problem solving techniques. This article seeks to draw a correlation between law school influences and later professional behavior.

Stone, Julius. Legal Education and Public Responsibility. Report and Analysis of the Conference On The Education of Lawyers For Their Public Responsibilities, 1956. Boulder, CO: Association of American Law Schools, 1959.

Explores the basic values embodied in the lawyer's trust and the role of legal education in developing them. Stone offers proposals for supplementing legal education including more intercourse between the practicing bar and the law school community, concentrated courses on ethics and a pervasive concern with ethical principles in all aspects of the law school curriculum.

Sutherland, Arthur E. The Law at Harvard. Cambridge: Belknap Press, 1967.

Recounts the contributions to the development of American law of such notable Harvard alumni as Story, Langdell, Ames, Thayer, Pound and contributions of the law school under the influence of recent deans.

Thode, E. Wayne and T.A. Smedley. "An Evaluation of the Pervasive Approach to Education for Professional Responsibility of Lawyers." University of Colorado Law Review 41 (1969), 365-372.

The pervasive approach to legal ethics training involves raising questions about attorneys' obligations in various professional contexts in all portions of the law school curriculum. This approach purports to sensitize students to ethical problems and make them aware of factors to be considered in dealing with them. The authors describe various ethical problems that might be confronted in a law curriculum.

Thurman, Samuel D. "The Legal Profession Course: An Evaluation." University of Colorado Law Review 41 (1969), 385-397.

Having examined the various kinds of legal profession courses taught in American law schools, Thurman suggests improvements. He discusses the goals, materials, advantages, shortcomings, teaching method and other aspects of an effective course in legal ethics.

Tuoni, Gilda M. "Teaching Ethical Considerations in the Clinical Setting, Professional, Personal and Systemic." University of Colorado Law Review 52 (1981), 409-418.

Discusses methods for introducing law students to ethical problems which arise in practice within the clinical legal education setting. Tuoni believes that clinical courses are well suited for confronting students with conflicts among ethical considerations, personal values and systemic values.

Watson, Andrew S. "The Watergate Lawyer Syndrome: An Educational Deficiency Disease." Journal of Legal Education 26 (1974), 441-448.

Discusses a psychiatric condition called the Watergate Syndrome which arises partly from deficiencies in legal education. The syndrome is a combination of ambition, loyalty and vanity that prevents the attorney from analyzing his actions from a moral and public-interest point of view. Watson concludes that education does not awaken the capacity to recognize the point at which self-interest begins to conflict with social and ethical concerns.

Weckstein, Donald T. "Watergate and the Law Schools." San Diego Law Review 12 (1975), 261-278.

Discusses Watergate's effects on and implications for legal education and suggests professional responsibility training. Weckstein states the useful and normal roles that legal education can perform are to identify and study problematic situations which give rise to legal ethics. He proposes a coordinated approach which would combine an introduction to philosophical and historical roles, problematical situations, the pervasive approach and clinics.

Weckstein, Donald T. "Legal Education In Professional Responsibility." The Encyclopedia of Education, ed. L. C. Deighton. New York: Macmillan, 1971, vol. 5, pp. 367-375.

Surveys and appraises various definitions of professional responsibility. Weckstein believes that much controversy could be eliminated by adopting a generally accepted definition. Since World War II law schools have increasingly emphasized professional responsibility. While most courses are not particularly effective, a pervasive and consistent approach has proved more effective.

Weckstein, Donald T. "Perspective Courses and Co-curricular Activities." University of Colorado Law Review 41 (1969), 398-429.

Examines perspective courses concerned with the development and function of legal institutions, and the role of law in protecting human dignity and diversity while attempting to provide for the common welfare. Such courses improve the student's capacity to perceive and make value choices. Weckstein supports co-curricular activities such as dicussion groups and faculty contact, speakers programs, moot courts and other informal activities that provide contact with various types of legal practice and attendant ethical concerns.

Weinstein, Jack, B. "On the Teaching of Legal Ethics." Columbia Law Review 72:3 (1972), 452-468.

Argues that education in ethics should be integrated into traditional law school curricula. Faculty should approach ethical issues from their own view of the role of the attorney in American society. Weinstein discusses particular ethical problems likely to be encountered in providing group legal services.

PART TWO

TOPICAL MATERIALS

CHAPTER THREE
THE LAWYER'S ROLE

A. GENERAL DISCUSSION

Black, Jonathan. "Lawyers on the Left: A Crisis of Identity." Village Voice, May 1, 1969.

Surveys radical law firms in New York, the cases they handle, the life styles their members lead and their differences in approach.

Blumberg, Abraham S., ed. The Scales of Justice. Chicago: Aldine Publishing Co., 1970.

Collection of articles reprinted from Transaction Magazine offering interdisciplinary consideration of the law and order issue in American society. Contributions discuss the role of the lawyer in protecting individual rights and the rights of the poor and minorities; and the tendency of American justice to work unfairness on the disadvantaged. All the articles show the view that the law and order issue is a result of middle-class prejudice and the political manipulation of middle-class fear and resentment.

Chemerinsky, Erwin. "Protecting Lawyers From Their Profession: Redefining the Lawyers' Role." Journal of the Legal Profession, 5 (1980), 31-43.

Discusses whether an attorney's personal beliefs should influence his professional conduct. Chemerinsky analyzes the implications for the lawyer's role of psychological studies on counter attitudinal advocacy, a theory which explains the unintended effects on beliefs of a person's efforts to persuade others. Chemerinsky argues lawyers should resist advocating positions that run counter to their personal beliefs. Lawyers would then considere that the social effects of their actions.

Flood, John. The Legal Profession in the United States. Chicago, IL: American Bar Foundation, 1984.

Presents an overview of lawyers' activities in practice and politics, social organization and education. Changes in the profession are discussed such as the introduction of advertising and the growth in large law firms. Flood outlines the direction in which the legal profession appears to be going. An annotated bibliography is included.

Freedman, Monroe. "Professional Responsibility of the Criminal Defense Lawyer: The Three Hardest Questions." Michigan Law Review, 64 (1966), 1469-1484.

Discusses three questions dealing with the lawyer's dilemma whether to betray confidential communication or to participate in purposeful deception of the court. First, is it proper to cross-examine for the purpose of discrediting an adverse witness whom the lawyer knows is telling the truth? Second, is it proper to allow a witness to commit perjury? Third, is it proper to give legal advice when the lawyer believes that the knowledge will tempt his client to commit perjury? The author answers all three questions affirmatively. Maintenance of an adversary system, presumption of innocence, the need to prove guilt beyond a reasonable doubt, the right to counsel, and lawyer-client confidentiality justify these answers.

Harvey, Brian W., ed. The Lawyer and Justice. London: Sweet and Maxwell, 1978.

Collection of addresses by distinguished jurists on law and the duties of lawyers. Topics include law and economics, judicial independence, law and civil life, the role of law in a democratic state, the role of the Lord Chancellor, judicial law-making and the scope and function of legal education

Horowitz, Harold W. and Kenneth L. Karot. Law, Lawyers and Social Change. New York: Bobbs Merril, 1969.

Introduces the American Legal system through cases and materials that show lawyers and the legal process involved in the movement for social change. Topics include consumer, housing and poverty law, new methods of providing legal services and the careers lawyers engaged in public interest practice.

Mayer, Martin. The Lawyers. New York: Harper and Row, 1966.

A journalistic-style survey of the legal profession describing generally how it functions; the process of training and specialization; and its function in civil, criminal and business law. The final section describes the court systems of the United States and considers the relationship between the bar and the bench and the development of law through the judicial process.

McGinn, Joseph C. *Lawyers: A Client's Manual*. Englewood Cliffs, NJ: Prentice-Hall, 1979.

Gives useful advice to lay persons by describing the function of an attorney in civil and criminal practice and suggesting under what circumstances legal services would be useful. McGinn discusses how to find a lawyer, fees, attorney liability, the nature of the attorney-client relationship, and attorney discipline.

Patterson, L. Ray. "Limits of the Lawyer's Discretion and the Law of Legal Ethics -- National Student Marketing Revisited." *Duke Law Journal*, 1979:6 (1979), 1251-1274.

Forecasts a change in lawyers' approach to ethical problems based on the National Student Marketing Corporation case. The lawyers represented two corporations in a merger in which proxy material showed a substantial profit. However, just before the merger closed, the corporate accountants informed the lawyers that, in fact, the profit was a net loss. Rather than publishing the loss, the lawyers proceeded with the merger. Patterson suggests that ethics are rules of law -- not morality; that the solution to ethical problems is in the rights and duties of the *client*, not the lawyer; and the determining factors are the nature of the client, the role of the lawyer and the legal process involved.

Riley, David. "Mystique of Lawyers." In *Verdicts on Lawyers*, eds. Ralph Nader and Mark Green. New York: Thomas Y. Crowell, 1976, pp. 80-93.

Discusses the traditional perception of lawyers as a class apart possessed of great power and influence in government and business. Riley believes that although lawyers' special knowledge of the legal system is relevant to political decisions about ordering society, legal expertise is not equivalent to a general wisdom about human affairs. Law is, in fact, dispensed by lawyers as a practical commodity. Regarding law as something more than a trade and failure to face its economic realities tends to minimize personal, emotional and ethical accountability by individual practitioners.

Silberman, Linda J. "Professional Responsibility Problems of Divorce Mediation." In Family Law Quarterly. 16:2 (Summer, 1982), 108-145. Reprinted in Ethics and the Legal Profession. eds. Frederick A. Elliston and Michael Davis. Buffalo, NY: Prometheus, 1984.

Assesses four different divorce mediation models in use around the country: (1) the single-lawyer mediator; (2) the solo therapist; (3) the lawyer-therapist team and; (4) the advisory-attorney variation. Silberman details the distinct set of issues raised and the professional responsibility problems of each model.

Smith, M. B. E. "Review Concerning Lawful Illegality: Kadish and Kadish, Discretion to Disobey. Yale Law Journal, 83 (1974), 1534-1549.

Argues that roles have the purpose of achieving a generalized and social goal. The rules governing role action are not explicit and though the means permitted are prescribed, the individual is aware of the end and may pursue it with non-prescribed means. The role itself thus contains the possibility of deviation. Smith finds the authors' views to be based on a flawed foundation in that they distinguish between legal and moral obligation and argue that legal obligations may not be moral obligations. Their method is thus unserviceable for discovering legal rules.

Wasserstrom, Richard. "Roles and Morality." From The Good Lawyer ed. David Luban. Totowa, NJ: Rowman & Allanheld, 1984, pp. 25-37.

Explores possible tensions between reasoning about how one should behave that is most unproblematically moral reasoning and another way of reasoning about how one should behave that, while also a kind of moral reasoning, occurs within the context and through the structure of familiar roles. Wasserstom seeks first to develop a critique of role-restricted reasoning about behavior in the light of the more universal aspects of morality. He then tries to identify a number of the more promiscuous responses that might be made to this critique. He concludes with some worries about roles that remain even after these responses are given.

B. ADVOCACY WITHIN THE ADVERSARIAL SYSTEM

American Bar Association. Chicago: Consortium For Professional Education. "Advocacy." Videotape (60 min.), Vignette (13 min.).

A defense attorney in a robbery and attempted rape case overhears the prosecuting attorney urge the victim to appear more certain of her identification of the defendant. The victim reveals she had been drinking on the night of the alleged crimes. The defense attorney uses this information in court and also employs other questionable tactics on behalf of his client. A panel discussion follows the vignette. This videotape raises several issues including the duties of the prosecutor, perjury, misuse of evidence, confidentiality, and fairness.

American Bar Association. Chicago: Consortium For Professional Education. "Negotiation." Videotape (60 min.), Vignette (13 min.).

A plaintiff's attorney, representing the parents of a young boy killed in an automobile accident, is not diligent in pursuing the case. He is unaware of a recent major change in the law favorable to his clients. In negotiation the defense counsel exploits the inexperience and incompetence of his adversary. Several issues are raised including attorney preparation, misrepresentation, attorney-client privilege, attorneys' duty to disclose criminal conduct, extortion, settlement tactics, and obligation to diligently represent every client.

Brown, Louise M., and Edward A. Dauer. <u>Planning by Lawyers: Materials on a Nonadversarial Legal Process</u>. Mineola, New York: Foundation Press, 1978.

Provides materials on preventive law -- the use of attorney's skills to avoid disputes and to structure relations and transactions. Such structuring requires legal planning which leads to the book's discussions of counseling, economic concerns, negotiation, and drafting documents. Practical applications in real property, business, family and insolvency are illustrated and explored.

Byrne, Edmund. "The Adversary System: Who Needs It?." In <u>Ethics and the Legal Profession</u> eds. Frederick A. Elliston and Michael Davis. Buffalo, NY: Prometheus, 1984.

Contends the American adversarial legal system is not working. Byrne attributes its failures to the system itself, either because it is wrongly applied to some kinds of cases or because it is structurally flawed in its original design. He draws this conclusion after rejecting the more favored theory that current difficulties are primarily procedural and can be solved by modifying procedures at points along the way.

Curtis, Charles P., "The Ethics of Advocacy." Stanford Law Review 4 (1951), 3-23.

Discusses the positive aspects of a lawyer's devotion to his client's cause. Curtis argues that there are times when a lawyer may lie or remain silent on his client's behalf. The ethics of advocacy are very much apart from the morals that govern individual behavior. The lawyer needs to pursue his duty no further than to make the best case possible for his client, for he takes his case as a case not a cause. Because he acts professionally and is personally detached from his client, no moral stigma attaches to him.

Donagan, Alan. "Justifying Legal Practice in the Adversary System." From The Good Lawyer ed. David Luban. Totowa, NJ: Rowman & Allanheld, 1984, pp. 123-149.

Explores two fundamental moral questions about legal practice in the adversary system. First, can such a practice be morally justified and if so under what conditions? Second, if there are conditions under which such practice is justified, does its justification impose further conditions on its conduct. Donagan outlines the conditions on any moral justification of the adversary system, cites the standard justifications for the system and explains their implications.

Dorsen, Norman. "Lawyers' Ethics in an Adversary System -- Freedman, M. H." Harvard Civil Rights and Civil Liberties Law Review 11:3 (1976), 764-769.

Interprets Freedman to claim the lawyer's duty is to help his client to prevail at all costs. Dorsenn highlights Freedman's analysis of the conduct of Richard Nixon's counsel and the controversy which ensued when counsel asserted that he was representing not the man, but the office of the Presidency.

Douglass, John J. Review of "Lawyers' Ethics in an Adversary System -- Freedman, M. H." Houston Law Review 14:2 (1977), 519-526.

Disparages the book's view that the adversary system is constitutionally mandated and the most effective means of protecting human dignity. This view, along with the book's elevation of the confidential nature of the lawyer-client privilege to constitutional status, wrongly supersedes an institutional commitment to truth, in Douglass's view.

Drinker, Henry S. "Some Remarks on Mr. Curtis' 'The Ethics of Advocacy.'" Stanford Law Review 4 (1952), 349-357.

Defends the integrity of the legal profession. Drinker argues that Curtis misinterprets Canon 15's prohibition against an attorney's assertion of his personal belief in the justice of his client's cause. The Canon requires that the client's case stand or fall on its own merit, not whether the counsel believes in it.

Ferren, John. "The Condlin-Redlich Exchange." From The Good Lawyer ed. David Luban. Totowa, NJ: Rowman & Allanheld, 1984, pp. 359-362.

Analyzes the disagreement between Condlin and Redlich and attributes it to their differing perceptions of the suitability of the adversary system to achieve the ends of justice. Ferren questions the ability of advocate supervisors of clinical experience to judge their case objectively.

Finally, he observes that continuous review of the adversary system is essential. Clinical legal education is an effort to teach professional responsibility, which is a career-long enterprise.

Frankel, Marvin E., "From Private Fights Toward Public Justice." New York University Law Review 51 (1976), 516-537.

The adversary model of justice is a product of the American values of individualism and competition. In this system public authorities have traditionally taken a passive, umpireal role in settling private disputes. Frankel urges authorities to take a stronger hand.

Frankel, Marvin. "The Search for Truth: An Umpireal View." <u>University of Pennsylvania Law Review</u> 123 (1975), 1031-1059.

Criticizes the adversary system because it rates truth too low and loyalty to the client too high. Compares the selection of trial judges from the ranks of experienced trial lawyers to the selection of former athletes as umpires. Discusses two unpromising approaches for controlling adversary excesses: 1) intervention by the judge; and 2) better training and regulation of counsel. In the first the judge as a participant is likely to impair the adversary process as often as he improves it. As for the second, Frankel argues that law students are trained all-too-well in obfuscating adverse facts and all-too-little in truth-seeking techniques. Alternatively, Frankel proposes 1) modifying the adversarial ideal; 2) making truth a paramount objective; and 3) imposing a duty to pursue that objective.

Freedman, Monroe H. "Are There Public Interest Limits in Lawyers' Advocacy?" <u>Journal of the Legal Profession</u> 2 (1977), 47-54.

Argues it violates public interest to restrain lawyers in advocacy and that only unrestricted advocacy produces an effective clash of opposing views. Though a lawyer has a duty to apprise a client that his claim is unjust, he may not make the ultimate decision to forego the suit.

Freedman, Monroe H. <u>Lawyers' Ethics in an Adversary System</u>. Indianapolis, IN: Bobbs-Merrill, 1975.

A classic that covers the nature of limitations on lawyer-client confidentiality and advocacy; the problems of the perjured client; impeaching a truthful witness; and ethical aspects of the prosecutorial function. Freedman discusses proposals for certification of trial lawyers and compares the British system of a bifurcated bar with that of the American bar.

Fried, Charles. "The Lawyer as Friend: The Moral Foundations of the Lawyer-Client Relation." <u>Yale Law Journal</u> 85 (1976), 1060-1089.

Evaluates two criticisms of the traditional conception of the lawyer as completely devoted to his client's interest to the point of doing some things for his client which he would not do for himself. First, professional loyalty to one's client is said to demand an allocation of the lawyer's time which does not always maximize the greatest good for the greatest number of people. Fried rebuts this criticism, saying that it is morally right that the lawyer advocate his client's interest ahead of the collective interest provided he offers good counsel. Second, advocacy is said to provide unfair advantages for the client while harming his adversary. Fried responds by stating that the lawyer is morally entitled to represent his client's interest, as long as he stays within the law and maintains his personal integrity.

Gilmore, Hon. Horace W. "Professional Responsibility Problems and Contempt in Advocacy." San Diego Law Review 12 (1975), 288-305.

Discusses appeals to the U.S. Supreme Court involving criminal contempt proceedings against attorneys for vigorous advocacy of their clients' causes. They show attorneys derive significant protection from the Sixth Amendment. Judge Gilmore points out that under the American Bar Association Code of Professional Responsibility Disciplinary Rules, a significantly lower standard applies in disciplinary proceedings arising out of undignified or discourteous conduct degrading to a tribunal, but not amounting to criminal contempt. He argues that the Sixth Amendment is satisfied with the standards under the Rules, and discusses the applicability of the Rules with respect to pre-trial publicity by an advocate.

Hegland, Kenney. "Moral Dilemmas in Teaching Trial Advocacy." Journal of Legal Education 32 (1982), 69-86.

Criticizes the overemphasis on winning in teaching the skills of advocacy and recommends restructuring these courses to bring about a critical and thoughtful examination of the lawyering process. This may involve less emphasis on the adversary nature of legal proceedings and more on reconciliation.

Kaufman, Irving R. "In Defense of the Advocate." University of California Los Angeles Law Review 12 (1965), 351-360.

Comments on a trend toward recognition of a right to be represented by effective counsel. Kaufman discusses methods by which the law student may develop skills as a trial attorney and elaborates upon the duty to develop those skills.

Kutak, Robert. "The Adversary System and the Practice of Law." From The Good Lawyer ed. David Luban. Totowa, NJ: Rowman & Allanheld, 1984, pp. 172-187.

The ABA Commission on Evaluation of Professional Standards sought coherent, workable solutions to the problem of confidentiality about client misconduct which would be in keeping with concepts basic to the American legal system. While recognizing that confidentiality is critical to the client-lawyer relationship, Kutak acknowledges that it is not without limitation. He argues that a lawyer can act as ethically as anyone else in the adversary system at large, and concludes that by expanding the concept of confidentiality and narrowing the exceptions for disclosure, the principle of confidentiality is strengthened in the general practice of law.

Lehman, Warren. "The Pursuit of a Client's Interest." Michigan Law Review 77 (1979), 1078-1097.

Argues that the view of an attorney as an instrument of the client's will in the context of the attorney-client relationship is simplistic because the attorney plays an active role in the client's decision. If the client wants something, the lawyer does not simply tell him how to get it. Rather, the lawyer is consulted as a man of practical wisdom - one who knows how to advance his client toward what is good, though not necessarily what the client originally wanted. The lawyer does this without manipulating his client.

Luban, David. The Adversary System Excuse. College Park, MD: Center for Philosophy and Public Policy, University of Maryland, 1981.

Discusses views of the adversary system. Luban concentrates on their means of justifying or not justifying the system, which may lead to morally objectionable results. He is especially critical of attorneys who employ morally reprehensible means, though santioned by the system, to help their clients prevail.

Noonan, John T. "Professional Ethics or Personal Responsibility?" Review of Lawyers' Ethics in an Adversary

System, by Monroe H. Freedman. Stanford Law Review 29 (1977), 363-370.

Rejoinder to Dean Freedman's Lawyer's Ethics in an Adversary System which criticizes Freedman's basic contentions: 1) that an honest person cannot practice as a criminal defense lawyer; 2) that a decent person cannot serve as a prosecutor; and 3) that an honest and decent person cannot teach law. Noonan believes these contentions were made because Freedman measures ethics by its systemic role rather than by its purposes, and because he believes professional ethics to be superior to personal ethics.

Noonan, John T. Jr. "The Purposes of Advocacy and the Limits of Confidentiality." Michigan Law Review 64 (1966), 1485-1482.

Treats absolute lawyer-client confidentiality as a barrier to truth and justice. Noonan criticizes Monroe Freedman's belief in absolute privilege because a lawyer is not simply a legal technician. Rather he should consider the requirements of the adversary system, his own standards as a human being, and the requirements of society when defending his client's interest.

Rich, William. "The Role of Lawyers: Beyond Advocacy." Brigham Young University Law Review 1980 (1980), 767-784.

Emphasizes that both lawyers and laymen must understand the potential of non-adversarial dispute resolution. This requires a re-appraisal of the attorney's function that emphasizes his role as a mediator between his client and the opposing party and de-emphasizes his traditional role as an advocate in litigation. Rich recommends that the proposed Model Rules of Professional Conduct facilitate this change.

Rogers, Showell. "The Ethics of Advocacy." Law Quartery Review 5 (1899), 259-280.

Rogers, writing almost a century ago, dismisses Jeremy Bentham's contention that a lawyer who defends a guilty criminal is culpable as an accessory after the fact. He agrees with Baron Bramwell and Dr. Johnson that the Court, after hearing arguments from both sides, can make a fair determination of justice. However, Rogers sets limits, stating that while the advocate can and should represent his client's interests, he may not misrepresent the facts. Rogers believes that lawyers carry out their role as advocates honorably.

Rubin, Alvin B. "A Causerie on Lawyers' Ethics in Negotiation." Louisiana Law Review 35 (1975), 577-593.

Notes that the vast majority of legal disputes, both civil and criminal, are resolved before trial. Rubin argues that the Code of Professional Responsibility does not adequately guide attorneys engaged in negotiations on behalf of clients. Obtaining the best possible settlement for one's client may mean that the attorney must misrepresent the extent of the client's injury or the weight of the evidence against his opponent. Rubin urges correcting this misapprehension.

Scardilli, Frank J. "Law, Lawyers and the Tyranny of Illusion." Humanist 41 (September-October 1981), 20-26.

Criticizes the myths that shroud the adversarial system. Scardilli recommends dispelling them by educating non-lawyers. He states that too much emphasis is placed on competition and the "winner-take-all" mentality, and recommends mediation as a more effective means of resolving disputes.

Schwartz, Murray. The Zeal of the Civil Advocate. College Park, MD: Center for Philosophy and Public Policy of the University of Maryland, 1982.

Examines the thesis that a lawyer is not legally, professionally or morally accountable for the means used to enable his client to prevail in civil litigation. Schwartz concludes that a lawyer does have a duty to reject a client's civil case if the client seeks a legal but immoral end. He then proposes a balancing test to weigh the right to representation in the objectionable cause, the probable injury to the other party, and the adequacy of representation of the cause without counsel. The court that applies this test may appoint counsel.

Shaffer, Thomas L. "Advocacy as Moral Discourse." North Carolina Law Review 57 (1979), 647-670.

Public interest advocacy is usually founded upon moral principles and is ineffective unless the parties are mutually open to the risk of persuasion. Moral discourse differs from adversary discourse in that it is interpersonal, argues from the person of the client, is addressed to the conscience of those who hear it, and is concilliatory in purpose.

Simon, William H. "The Ideology of Advocacy: Procedural Justice and Professional Ethics." Wisconsin Law Review 1978 (1978), 29-144.

Discusses the ideology of advocacy as the profession's defense to public criticism of its morally neutral stance and evaluates three justifications. On the Hobbesian view, individuals are entitled to use whatever means are necessary to achieve their own ends. On the Positivists' view, law is regarded as a technical apparatus for the advancement of social norms. On the ritualist view, adversary proceedings are a public ceremony designed to show that something is being accomplished. Simon discusses procedural limitations on all three.

Singley, Carl E. Review of Lawyers' Ethics In An Adversary System, by Monroe H. Freedman. University of Pittsburgh Law Review 38 (1976), 135-143.

Freedman's solutions to some ethical dilemmas encountered in legal practice are criticized as sophistic. His annotations to the Code of Professional Responsibility share with the Code a failure to anticipate emerging ethical problems caused by the changing nature of criminal defense advocacy. Singley takes issue with Freedman's proposition that an advocate's only responsibility is to his client, arguing that it opens the profession to strident moral criticisms. Singley argues that Freedman's view is simplistic and that he ascribes too much ethical homogeneity to American lawyers as a group.

Taylor, Allen. "The Adversary System of Justice: An Ethical Jungle." Journal of Critical Analysis 3 (April 1971), 23-28.

Considers the lawyer's ethical dilemma of choosing between his duty to the client and his duty to the court. Taylor discusses various perspectives including Monroe Freedman's and the American Bar Association's. He concludes that if an attorney's job is to help produce a rational and informed decision, he should not abet perjury or attack truthful witnesses. He recommends restricting the priviledge of confidentiality and overhauling the adversary system.

Thurman, Samuel D. "Limits to the Adversary System: Interests That Outweigh Confidentiality." Journal of the Legal Profession 5 (1980), 5-19.

Defines the adversary system and discusses some limitations necessary to insure that the process produces correct results. Thurman deals with counsel's right to withdraw where a client cannot be dissuaded from pursuing an unjust end; conflicts of interest in proceeding against the interests of a former client; the requirement that counsel reveal client confidences necessary to prevent a crime; duties to corporate clients that may involve disclosure of confidences made by corporate employees; and the duty to reveal a client's perjury.

C. THE LAWYER-CLIENT RELATIONSHIP

Burt, Robert A. "Conflict and Trust Between Attorney and Client." Georgia Law Journal 69 (April 1981), 1015-1046.

Argues that mistrust pervades attorney-client relations though practical incentives and professional norms lead both parties to resist admitting it. Burt criticizes the pending proposals regarding disclosure of client communications in the Model Rules of Professional Conduct for exacerbating this problem and recommends more stringent disclosure requirements to prompt attorney-client explorations of mistrust.

Butler, Stephen J. "Rule Prohibiting an Attorney from Testifying at a Client's Trial - Ethical Paradox." University of Cincinnati Law Review 45:2 (1976), 268-273.

Discusses the Canons of the Americaan Bar Association Code of Professional Responsibility which prohibit an attorney from testifying as a witness in a case in which he is an advocate. Butler criticizes the rationale for this rule, suggesting that the code is more concerned with the appearance of impropriety than substantive justice.

Casper, Jonathan D. "Improving Defender-Client Relations." NLADA [National Legal Aid and Defender Association] Briefcase 34:4 (Aug. 1977), 114-116, 126-131.

Factors related to the tendency of defendants to distrust public defenders are explored in an analysis of data obtained in 812 postarrest and 628 postdisposition interviews with men charged with felonies. The interviews took place in Phoenix, Baltimore and Detroit. The data suggest that defendants are much more distrustful of public defenders than they are of private lawyers. Tabular data are included.

Danet, Brenda, Kenneth B. Hoffman and Nicole C. Rermish. "Obstacles to the Study of Lawyer-Client Interaction: the Biography of Failure." Law and Society Review 14 (1980), 905-922.

An interdisciplinary team attempted to observe and record lawyer-client interactions to determine the means to achieve greater accountability of attorneys to the public. The reasons for the failure of the attempt, including the obstacle of the attorney-client privilege, are discussed.

Frankel, Charles. "Review of the Code of Professional Responsibility of the American Bar Association." University of Chicago Law Review 43 (1976), 874-886.

Criticizes the fact that a number of ethical problems that might well have been drafted as disciplinary rules appear as ethical considerations. Frankel suspects that the draftsmen had little faith in the disciplinary procedures available to the bar and thus cast difficult problems of interpretation as ethical considerations. He argues that implicit in the Code is the attitude that its purpose is to sensitize the profession to the scope and complexity of their professional obligations rather than to function as a list of proscribed activities. Frankel faults the authors for not making the rationale explicit.

Gillers, Stephen. Rights of Lawyers and Clients. New York: Avon Books, 1979.

This handbook, published in cooperation with the American Civil Liberties Union, sets forth in question-and-answer format the legal rights and responsibilities of attorneys and their clients. It reviews issues pertaining to admission to the bar, covering such areas as applicants' rights to see their bar exam papers, the legality of loyalty oaths, character committees, and the power to exclude applicants with criminal records. Also discussed are issues related to the admission to practice, and special procedural issues including constitutional rights at a disciplinary meeting, the burden of proof, presumptions and the relationship between disciplinary proceedings and the privilege against self-incrimination. The attorney-client privilege and the nature of lawyers' fiduciary relationship to their client are examined. Questions related to conflict of interest, attorneys' fees and liens, and attorney malpractice are also considered. Two appendices are included on State bar admission requirements and Federal statutes authorizing award of attorneys' fees.

Landsman, Stephan. "The Decline of the Adversary System and The Changing Role of the Advocate in that System." San Diego Law Review 18 (1981), 251-261.

Argues that the ABA's Model Rules of Professional Conduct challenge the adversary system's emphasis on zealous advocacy. Landsman suggests their adoption would interferes with a lawyer's ability to effectively perform in the judicial process. This would threaten the entire adversary system and the rights it vindicates.

"The Lawyer as Friend." Letter. Yale Law Journal 86 (1977), 573-587.

Correspondence to the editors critical of Charles Fried's article "The Lawyer as Friend: the Moral Foundation of the Lawyer-Client Relation." The author argues that the friendship analogy is misleading because the relation between a lawyer and his client aims at achieving different sorts of benefits for both than does a relationship between friends. It is well not to invest the former with characteristics of the latter in order to explain reality.

Leubsdorf, John. "Communicating With Another Lawyer's Client: The Lawyer's Veto and the Client's Interests." University Pennsylvania Law Review 127 (1979), 683-710.

The Code of Professional Responsibility forbids a lawyer to communicate directly with a represented party without permission of the party's lawyer. Leubsdorf argues that this veto power is not in the client's best interest because it results in indirect communication, higher fees and makes it easier for lawyers to neglect or deceive their clients. He suggests modifying the rule so that the communicating attorneys must identify themselves and their client and notify the other parties that they have a right to secure counsel before speaking. This would give the client the ultimate authority to decide whether to communicate.

Losey, Joseph, director. King and Country. With Dirk Bogarde and Tom Courtenay. B. H. E. Productions, 1966.

Story of an English soldier accused of desertion. His military attorney, at first unsympathetic, eventually yields to his client's sincerity and pleas for leniency. However, the court's interest in maintaining military discipline sends the soldier to a firing squad.

Mazor, Lester J. "Power and Responsibility in the Attorney-Client Relation." Stanford Law Review 20 (1968), 1120-1139.

Describes situations in which attorney default, negligence, or malpractice result in clients' liability and traditional remedies against the attorney. Such remedies have proliferated as a result of the court's recognition of the right to effective counsel. Mazor regards this as an historic shift in the allocation of power and responsibility in the attorney-client relation.

Pound, Roscoe. Law and Morals. 2nd Ed. Chapel Hill, NC: University of North Carolina Press, 1926.

Discusses historical, analytical and philosophical views of the relationship between law and morals.

Pound, Roscoe. "Justice According to the Law." Columbia Law Review 13 (1913), 696-713.

A 70-year old essay, still timely, that contrasts the legal and non-legal administration of justice. The latter, justice without law, works well in an agricultural society whereas in a complex commercial society, justice with law is useful. It makes justice predictable, protects against misjudgment and improper motive, provides standards and precedents and secures a long-term perspective. Yet it tends to be impersonal, to become an end in itself, to multiply law unnecessarily, and to frustrate judicial frontiers.

Redmount, Robert S. "New Dimensions of Professional Responsibility." Journal of the Legal Profession 3 (1978), 43-56.

Criticizes the policy of allowing the legal profession to define its own responsibility because it results in considerable autonomy and power in subordinating clients' needs. Redmont proposes reorienting professional attitudes to recognize the needs of individual clients.

Rosenthal, Douglas E. Lawyer and Client: Who's in Charge? New York: Russell Sage Foundation, 1974.

A study of personal injury lawyers and how their clients evaluate them. Rosenthal discusses models of the professional-client relationship, client participation, the nature of personal injury problems, conflicts of interest between lawyer and client in personal injury litigation, client access to effective legal services and principles and policies governing relations between professional and client relationships.

Spiegel, Mark. "Lawyering and Client Decision Making: Informed Consent and the Legal Profession." University Pennsylvania Law Review 128 (1979), 41-140.

The doctrine of consent requires that a physician inform a patient of possible consequences of medical treatment prior to obtaining the patient's consent. Spiegel advocates applying a similar doctrine to the attorney-client relationship which would limit the danger of attorney domination of clients. He describes the rise of the doctrine in medical malpractice cases and discusses its analogs in civil cases involving lawyers.

Thode, E. Wayne. "Canons 6 and 7: The Lawyer-Client Relationship." Texas Law Review 48 (1970), 367-379.

Examines the requirements of attorney competence and representation with zeal within the bounds of the law. Thode believes that the canons set the proper standards in these two areas, but that the disciplinary procedures provided by the Code are unworkable.

D. CONFLICT OF INTEREST

American Bar Association. Consortium For Professional Education. "Interviewing and the Lawyer-Client Relationship." Videotape (60 minutes).

A couple approach an attorney who is their mutual friend and ask him to represent them both in their divorce action. The attorney already represents the husband's employer. In addition to the probable conflict of interest, problems arise concerning property settlement, custody, and legal fees.

Comment. "A Dilemma in Professional Responsibility: the Subsequent Representation Problem." <u>Journal of Missouri-Kansas City Law Review</u> 50 (1982), 165-181.

Discusses the circumstances under which a court may disqualify an attorney who has previously represented one of the adverse parties. Such disqualification is appropriate only where there is a substantial relationship between the present controversy and the matter in which the attorney represented the adverse party. The author criticizes the courts' tendency to extend this test to include more than an obvious conflict of interest, arguing that the proper function of the standard is to protect client confidences made during the former association with opposing counsel.

Comment. "Ethical Concerns of Lawyers Who are Related by Kinship or Marriage." <u>Oregon Law Review</u> 60 (1981), 399-411.

The ABA Code of Professional Responsibility provides little guidance for lawyers to avoid conflict of interest problems based on kinship or marriage to opposing counsel. The author outlines the nature of the ethical issues raised and suggests methods by which such conflicts may be avoided.

Cross, John J. "Ethical Issues Facing Lawyer-Spouses and Their Employers." <u>Vanderbilt Law Review</u> 34 (1981), 1435-1462.

In <u>Blumenfeld v. Borenstein</u>, the Georgia Supreme Court dealt with the ethical problem raised when attorneys who are husband and wife represent opposing parties. This comment discusses the case and the applicable provisions of the Code of Professional Responsibility. The Court held that actual impropriety must be shown in such a case, not the public perception of impropriety arising solely from the marital status of the attorneys.

Davis, Michael. "Conflict of Interest." Business and Professional Ethics Journal, 1:1 (1982), 17-27.

Response to Joseph Margolis's article "Conflict of Interest and Conflicting Interests. Davis credits Margolis with being the first in business and profession ethics to raise the theoretical problem of conflict of interest. But he faults Margolis for failure to draw on the theory developed in the relevant legal literature. Margolis analyzed conflict of interest as an avoidable exploiting of conflicting roles. The literature on legal ethics, Davis contends, long ago developed an analysis of conflict of interest as a situation tending to undermine independent professional judgment. The legal ethics analysis is different and better because it connects conflict of interest with undermined judgment within a role rather than with conflict between roles. Davis warns others to refer to the literature on legal ethics before writing about problems on business and professional ethics.

"Developments in the Law -- Conflicts of Interest in the Legal Profession." Harvard Law Review 94 (April 1981), 1244-1503.

Discusses conflicts of interest in private practice, criminal law, poverty litigation, government and public interest law. Concludes with a discussion of sanctions and civil remedies available to deal with violations of the Code of Professional Ethics and the rights of clients.

Enker, Arnold N. "The Rationale of the Rule that Forbids a Lawyer to be Advocate and Witness in the Same Case." American Bar Foundation Research Journal 1977 (1977), 455-465.

Argues that the disciplinary rules prohibiting a lawyer from appearing as a witness in a trial in which he is counsel are founded upon the need to protect the attorney's professional role. That role is unique and depends upon the attorney's independence from his client so that the finder of fact will decide the rights of the parties by reason rather than emotion.

Geer, J. S. "Representation of Multiple Criminal Defendants: Conflicts of Interest and the Professional Responsibilities of the Defense Attorney." Minnesota Law Review 62:2 (1978), 119-162.

Discusses conflicts of interest at various stages of a criminal proceeding and relative to various aspects of trial representation. Geer argues that the defense lawyer representing more than one defendant is continually called upon to make choices between the interests of one client over another. All means of minimizing the ill-effects of multiple representation are criticized. Geer recommends amending the Code of Professional Responsibility to prohibit multiple representation in criminal cases.

Kindregan, Charles P. "Conflict of Interest and the Lawyer in Civil Practice." Valparaiso University Law Review 10 (1976), 423-452.

Discusses conflict of interest problems and their resolution in a variety of contexts such as conflict between lawyer and client interests and an attorney's acting as a witness, administrator or public official under apparently improper circumstances. Kindregan views frank communication between attorney and client as a prophylactic for such a conflict situation.

Kipnis, Kenneth. "Conflict of Interest and Conflict of Obligation." In Legal Ethics. Englewood Cliffs, NY: Prentice Hall, 1984. Reprinted in Ethics and the Legal Profession eds. Frederick A. Elliston and Michael Davis. Buffalo, NY: Prometheus, 1984.

Notes that the term 'conflict of interest' is highly ambiguous because it denotes two different circumstances. Kipnis endeavors to distinguish among the different kinds of conflicts of interest and to isolate what is ethically interesting in each of them.

Kizer, John O. "Legal Ethics and the Prosecuting Attorney." West Virginia Law Review 79 (1977), 367-380.

West Virginia permits county prosecutors to engage in private practice. Kizer discusses possible conflicts of interest that might arise as a result of this practice and outlines the requirements of the applicable provisions of the Code of Professional Responsibility.

Midonick, Millard L. "Attorney-Client Conflicts and Confidences in Trusts and Estates." Record of New York City Bar Association 35 (April 1980), 215-226.

Deals with the unique ethical problems facing the trust and estates bar: the duty of non-disclosure of confidences imparted by deceased clients; conflicts in interspousal litigation from possessing confidential financial information concerning both spouses; and the risk of self-dealing and overreaching in the administration of estates.

Note. "Unchanging Rules in Changing Times. The Canons of Ethics and Intra-firm Conflicts of Interest." Yale Law Journal 73 (1964), 1058-1079.

Notes a discrepancy between the Canon's proscription against attorneys or their firms representing a client who formerly employed the attorney and the fact that the proscription is frequently ignored. The author advocates a more flexible rule of disqualification where no former attorney-client confidences are endangered in the current dispute.

Oatway, Francis C. "Motivation and Responsibility in Tax Practice: The Need For Definition." Tax Law Review 20 (1965), 237-257.

Discusses ethical problems arising in the practice of tax law where the attorney may owe a duty both to the government and his client. Oatway argues that there is as yet little guidance provided for attorneys facing ethical dilemmas which arise from assisting a client in minimizing tax liability.

Stern, Jeffrey. "Dilemmas For Insurance Counsel - Coping With Conflicts of Interest." Massachusetts Law Review 65 (1980), 127-132.

Discusses conflict of interest issues that arise where counsel represents both the insuror and the insured. Such relationships threaten the confidences of both parties. Stern discusses cases in which counsel took steps to protect the insuror from possible claims against it by the insured while counsel engaged in the defense of the insured. The courts have condemned such conduct. Nonetheless, the ethical breaches have been only indirectly addressed by the courts and adequate guidance has not been provided.

Wice, Brian William. "Representation of Multiple Criminal Defendants: Conflicts of Interest and the Responsibility of the Defense Lawyer." Texas Bar Journal 44 (July 1981), 729-736.

Representation of multiple criminal defendants by a single attorney may have serious consequences as a violation of a defendant's constitutional rights and a breach of professional responsibility. Wice discusses indicators of a significant conflict of interest of which a defense attorney should be cognizant in order to avoid these consequences.

E. PUBLIC INTEREST

American Bar Association. Special Committee on Public Interest Practice. Implementing the Lawyer's Public Interest Practice Obligation. June 1977.

Discusses public interest roles for lawyers in different practices. Seeks to further the bar's policy of aiding all attorneys in carrying out their responsibility to provide free or low-cost public interest legal services relating to poverty, civil rights, public rights, charitable organizations and the administration of justice.

Atwood, John W. "Professional Responsibility and the Organized Bar -- An Essay On the Role of the Lawyer as a Social Engineer." Nebraska Law Review 51:3 (Spring 1972), 421-455.

Considers the right of the profession in the 70s, the meaning of canon eight of the Code of Professional Responsibility and its relationship to the role of the lawyer as a social engineer. Atwood recommends that legal education emphasize a lawyers public interest obligation and acquaint law students with the practical aspects of the law.

Auerbach, Jerold S. Unequal Justice: Lawyers and Social Change in Modern America. New York: Oxford University Press, 1976.

Discusses the role of the legal profession in effecting social change and traces developments in the profession such as specialization, government service and social activism. Stratification of bar membership and the role of self-regulation are considered and criticized. Auerbach concludes that the profession has been unresponsive to social change and that a reorientation toward the needs of society is necessary. Contains extensive documentation and a bibliographical essay.

Bellow, Gary and Jeann Kettleson. "From Ethics to Politics: Confronting Scarcity and Fairness in Public Interest Practice." Boston University Law Review 58 (May 1978), 337-390.

Explores several of the most persistent ethical dilemmas of public interest firms: how to service all clients with pressing legal problems; how to avoid overextending their limited resources; whether to disclose unlawful acts by disadvantaged clients; and whether to proceed against an economically disadvantaged adversary.

Bellow, Gary and Jeann Kettleson. "Mirror of Public Interest Ethics -- Problems and Paradoxes." Teaching Professional Responsibility: Materials and Proceedings from the National Conference ed. Patrick A. Keenan et al. Detroit, MI: University of Detroit School of Law, 1979.

The emergence of a public interest bar reflects and responds to longstanding tensions between a lawyer's obligations to clients and those to the public generally. As more groups and interests seek representation within the legal system, lawyers find themselves at the center of conflicts. Eventually the entire bar will have to confront the issues of professional responsibility that the public-interest lawyer has begun to bring into focus. It is not client demand, but program-defined noneconomic criteria that determine the content and character of representation. Distinctive problems of public attorneys include deciding who gets the allotted services and representation from the limited resources of the public interest firm and what obligations are still owed to those who are turned away. The authors urge the bar to increase services to the disadvantaged, and deal with the dilemmas created by scarcity. Examples of public interest cases and footnotes are provided.

Cahn, Edmund. The Moral Decision: Right and Wrong in the Light of American Law. Bloomington,IN: Indiana University Press, 1955.

Discusses morality and the legal order, distinguishing between law and morality and how they appear in legislation and judicial law-giving. Cahn traces the relationship between morality and law in matters of life, sexual relationships, business with government and personal fulfillment. He discusses the moral aspects of American procedural justice, emphasizing judicial interpretation of the law.

Cann, Wesley A. "Frivolous Lawsuits -- the Lawyer's Duty To Say 'No'." University of Colorado Law Review 52 (1981), 367-391.

Discusses the sources of a lawyer's duty to refrain from instituting frivolous law suits and the potential liability of a lawyer who does so. The duty to say "No" arises from the obligation to reflect credit upon the profession, to abide by specific provisions of the code and from the duty to uphold the legal system. Cann discusses the relevant provisions of the proposed Rules of Professional Conduct.

Capwell, Rex and Herbert Terwilliger. "Specialization? Pro and Con." Wisconsin Bar Bulletin 54:2 (1981), 17-18, 69-72.

Presents arguments for and against the adoption of a state-regulated plan to insure the existence of a lawyer's claimed specialized competence. The argument for the plan is that it is necessary to insure that consumers have accurate information available. The argument against it is it would be impossible to administer and would not ultimately benefit the consumer.

Carlin, Jerome E. Lawyers' Ethics: A Survey of the New York City Bar. New York: Russell Sage Foundation, 1966.

Reports the results of a survey of members of the New York City Bar to determine lawyer's attitudes toward ethical problems that arise in the context of the practice of law. Carlin examines the social structure of the bar and attempts to relate status differences to ethical norms. He also examines attitudes towards client relations, contacts with the courts, government agencies and the organized bar. He describes the formal controls for professional discipline within the bar and lawyers' attitudes towards them.

Carr-Saunders, A. M., and P. A. Wilson. The Professions. London: Frank Cass and Co., 1964.

Describes various professions in England and Wales, comparing their organizations, and speculates on their future role in society.

Ferren, John M. "The Corporate Lawyer's Obligation to the Public Interest." Business Lawyer, 33 (March 1978), 1253-1289.

Discusses the particular ethical problems faced by corporate counsel given inside information, which the company seeks to suppress, that a company product may pose a danger to the public. Discusses counsel's obligations before and after a defect-related disaster with respect to varied echelons of the corporate client.

Garrett, Ray Jr. "The Social Responsibility of Lawyers in Their Professional Capacity." University of Miami Law Review, 30 (1976), 879-913.

Discusses the duties of attorneys in securities regulation to make adequate investigations to determine the truthfulness of all matters requiring full disclosure. This system relies upon the proper behavior of attorneys. However, it is not clear that an attorney in this milieu has a social responsibility that must prevail over the interests of the client. Garrett argues the attorney's primary social responsibility is to provide guidance to clients that would enable them to comply with the law.

Gibson, William W. Jr. "American Bar Association Code Canon 5 -- Professional Judgment." Texas Law Review 48 (1970), 351-366.

Discusses ethical considerations and disciplinary rules relating to conflicting interests of lawyers, clients, and third persons that might prevent counsel from giving independent professional judgment. Gibson criticizes the Code's concept of "client consent" as not workable because attorneys should exercise their own professional judgment when conflicts arise.

Nader, Ralph M. "The Legal Profession: A Time for Self-Analysis." Akron Law Review 13 (1979), 1-18.

Views justice as continually embattled in a struggle with power. Nader believes legal constraints on power are ineffective unless representation is adequate and remedies are legally enforceable. Lack of knowledge and method may obstruct representation. He believes the legal profession should overcome the obstacles and provide adequate representation to the public, citing the Equal Justice Foundation as an example.

F. THE CORPORATE LAWYER

American Bar Association. Consortium For Professional Education. "Counseling." Videotape (60 min.), Vignette (8 min.).

The president of a major corporation has summoned his general counsel to discuss certain disclosure problems related to the corporation's forthcoming securities registration. He is also concerned about a product liability suit which may cause corporate bribes to be revealed. The vignette is followed by a panel discussing Corporation Law, Securities, Products Liability, and Agency.

Burke, Maureen H. "The Duty of Confidentiality and Disclosing Corporate Misconduct." Business Lawyer, 36 (Jan. 1981), 239-295.

Summarizes state, federal and professional proposals for clarifying an attorney's duty to disclose the wrongdoing of his or her corporate client. The American Bar Association's Model Rules of Professional Conduct is extensively discussed. Burke concludes that clarification must be the combined result of efforts by corporations, corporate law firms, regulatory agencies and bar associations.

Coomb, Jr. George W. "Multinational Codes of Conduct and Corporate Accountability: New Opportunities for Corporate Counsel." Business Lawyer, 36 (1981), 11-43.

Multinational codes of conduct were adopted in the wake of illicit payments overseas and election law violations by corporations at home. They provide corporate counsel with a new perspective in helping management address public expectations of corporate conduct.

"Ethical Responsibilities of Corporate Lawyers: Proceedings of the Airlie House Conference, June 9-11, 1977, Airlie, Virginia." Business Lawyer, 33 (March 1978), 1173-1586.

Papers on the nature of problems unique to corporate practice: responsibilities for opinions, public documents, illegal or fraudulent acts by clients, limitations on counsel's freedom to serve the public interest, the propriety of corporate counsel also sitting on the board of directors, and a critique of the effectiveness of bar efforts to make corporate practitioners aware of the need to be sensitive to problems of professional responsibility.

Forrow, Brian D. "The Corporate Law Department Lawyer: Counsel to the Entity." Business Lawyer, 34 (1979), 1797-1830.

Describes the duties and responsibilities of inside counsel and the requirements of the Code of Professional Responsibility in his or her dealings with directors, officers, and shareholders of the corporation, outside counsel and regulatory agencies. Sections deal with patents, anti-trust violations, bribing of foreign officials, product liability and environmental law. Forrow points out that many of the most able practitioners are in corporate practice.

Frank, Harvey. "A Higher Duty: a New Look at the Ethics of the Corporate Lawyer." Cleveland State Law Review, 26 (1977), 337-364.

Discusses amendments to the Code of Professional Responsibility prompted by policy developments of the SEC and the courts. Specifically, Frank discusses proposals to require attorneys to disclose client misconduct by informing their client's officers and board members of his reasons and intentions. Frank also discusses revised guidelines for an attorney's responsibility to shareholders.

Free, William J. "It's Not Who You Are But What You Know: Corporate Attorney-Client Privilege Expanded." (UpJohn Co. v. U.S., 66 L.Ed. 2d. 584, 1981) Oklahoma Bar Journal, 52 (28 March 1981), 701-703.

Discusses Upjohn Co. v. United States 101 S. Ct. in which the Supreme Court addressed the problem of identifying the communications with a corporate client that are protected by the attorney-client privilege. The court denied that it was adopting a general rule, but Free points out that it found the "control group" test inadequate and suggested that a broader class of communications to corporate counsel should be regarded as privileged.

Greenhouse, Linda. "In Corporate Law, Who's the Client?" New York Times. sec. 4, p. 20, col. 3. Feb. 15, 1981.

Examines the ambiguity of lawyer-client relationships in corporate law, noting that the American Bar Association's revised Code of Professional Responsibility has been criticized for failing to deal with problems of corporate practice. Greenhouse discusses the controversy over the new draft of the code which would require lawyers to "blow the whistle" on corporations if highest levels of management are implicated in possible wrongdoing.

Gross, Kent. "Attorneys and Their Corporate Clients: SEC Rule 2 (E) and the Georgetown 'Whistle Blowing' Proposal." Corporation Law Review, 3 (Summer 1980), 197-227.

In May of 1978 the Institute for Public Interest Representation, affiliated with Georgetown University Law Center, petitioned the SEC to define the responsibilities of an attorney who discovered that a client had perpetrated a fraud on the SEC or any individual. In November 1978, the Institute sought a requirement that the attorney disclose securities law violations to the corporate Board of Directors. Gross suggests that the Bar itself promulgate guidelines as to when a report to the Board is required.

Hershman, M. "The Murky Divide -- Professionalism and Professional Responsibility -- Business Judgment and Legal Advice -- What is a Business Lawyer?" Business Lawyer, 31:1 (1975), 457-463.

Summarizes a panel discussion on the professional responsibility of business lawyers and the murky divide between sound business judgment and astute legal advice. Hershman focuses mainly on problems of the attorney's role when representing a multinational U.S. corporation which has made secret payments to a foreign intermediary in return for favorable consideration. Should he resign or "blow the whistle" on moral grounds? Two opposing views emerge. The first requires resignation while the second permits individual discretion depending on the circumstances.

Hoffman, Junius. "On Learning of a Corporate Client's Crime or Fraud: The Lawyer's Dilemma." *Business Lawyer*, 33 (March 1978), 1389-1431.

The lawyer's duty to disclose -- or not disclose -- his corporate client's crime or fraud often requires weighing a number of competing considerations. The conflicts in the canons of the American Bar Association Code of Professional Responsibility primarily concern protection of the client's interest and the lawyer's responsibility to other segments of society.

Leary, Thomas B. "Is There a Conflict in Representing a Corporation and its Individual Employees?" *Business Lawyer*, 36 (1981), 591-595.

Discusses possible conflicts that may arise when a lawyer represents both a corporation and its employees. Prosecutors fear collusion or later reversal based on the defendant's failure to knowingly waive the conflict situation. Leary argues against imposing a presumption against joint representation since in many cases, one may not separate the corporation from its employees. If the attorney may not have access to the employees, he is disabled from representing the corporation. A panel discussion of the issue follows.

Lorne, Simon M. "The Corporate and Securities Adviser, the Public Interest, and Professional Ethics (The Lawyer Who Functions Primarily as an Adviser Rather Than in the Traditional Role of Advocate)." *Michigan Law Review*, 76 (Jan. 1978), 423-496.

Addresses the question of whether the corporate advisor's present role as confidant of management, exercising independent judgment and moral persuasion to affect client behavior, should be changed to a role independent of management, with primary loyalty to the general public. Lorne focuses on securities lawyers, but suggests that other practitioners whose function is primarily advisory will be affected by developments in this area.

Luban, David. Corporate Counsel and Confidentiality. College Park, MD: Center for Philosophy and Public Policy, University of Maryland, 1981.

Appraises the moral justification for whistleblowing generally acceptable to the public: there is a severe danger; the perpetrator is well aware of it; the whistleblower is motivated by moral concern; and the act is not retributive. Luban uses the case of the Ford Pinto fuel tank deficiencies to explore the duties of corporate counsel and concludes that counsel should disclose whether his or her client's behavior is ethical.

Maupin, Michael W. "Environmental Law, the Corporate Lawyer and the Model Rules of Professional Conduct." Business Lawyer, 36 (1981), 431-460.

Examines several of the Model Rules having particular significance to environmental lawyers. Maupin concludes that the proposed rules would impose an obligation on lawyers to make technical and scientific judgments that they may not be competent to make and that would discourage client confidences in some cases. Nonetheless, the Rules do provide guidance in identifying judgments the lawyers must make.

Note. "The Corporate Attorney-Client Privilege: Culpable Employees, Attorney Ethics, and the Joint Defense Doctrine." Texas Law Review, 58 (1980), 809-843.

Describes the development and scope of the corporate attorney-client privilege. The author proposes the formulation of a corporate evidentiary privilege for communications by employees to corporate counsel.

Note. "Should Lawyers Serve as Directors of Corporations For Which They Act as Counsel?" Utah Law Review, 1978 (1978), 711-740.

Examines the conflict of interests aspect of an attorney's service as a director of a client corporation. The author concludes that an attorney's ethical duty is to undertake such service only if he is convinced that the corporate and societal benefits flowing from their dual service exceed the respective burdens created by their conflicting duties.

"Proceedings of the Arlie House Conference: Ethical Responsibilities of Corporate Lawyers." Business Lawyer, 33 (1978), 1173-1586.

Contains panel discussions held during a conference on ethical responsibilities. Topics include corporate clients' expectations of counsel, conflict problems, counsel's responsibility for clients' actions and to the public interest, service by counsel on boards of directors, and discussion of whether the Code of Professional Resonsibility adequately sensitizes the corporate bar to its ethical obligations.

Rotunda, Ronald D. "Law, Lawyers and Managers." In Ethical Theory and Business. Ed. Tom L. Beauchamp and Norman A. Bowie. Englewood Cliffs, NJ: Prentice-Hall, 1979, pp. 317-324.

Discusses corporate legal ethics, identifying two major conflicts of interest. The first deals with corporate lawyers and managers who represent diverse interests within an organization. The author recommends tightening the rules to bar lawyers from serving on boards of their clients and not allowing corporate clients to employ lawyers from their boards. The second concerns the duties of corporate lawyers and managers to outside interests. Author recommends not allowing lawyers to bill private clients for outside professional time, and concludes that the separation of public and private capacities is a basic ethical necessity.

Rueschemeyer, Dietrick. Lawyers and Their Society: A Comparative Study of the Legal Profession in Germany and the United States. Cambridge: Harvard University Press, 1973.

This is a study of the bar in private practice in Germany and the U.S.. The author discusses the profession's role in society regarding sociological theory such as values consensus and power, and social integration and conflict as they affect social order and change. Views on professional ethics in both countries are discussed in a separate chapter.

Slovak, Jeffrey S. "The Ethics of Corporate Lawyers: A Sociological Approach." American Bar Foundation Research Journal, 1981 (1981), 753-794.

Offers a sociological perspective on a corporate counsel's public disclosure of organizational wrongdoing. The act of disclosure is treated as predictable social behavior. The author describes the factors leading to prediction of disclosure and discusses ramifications of the proposed revisions of the American Bar Association Code of Professional Ethics.

Smigel, Erwin O. The Wall Street Lawyer: Professional Organization Man?" Bloomington, IN: Indiana University Press, 1969.

Reports on the impact of large law firms upon the lawyer, his clients and ultimately upon the law itself. The author describes patterns of recruitment selection of lawyers and the organization of big law firms. He discusses the ethical and policy dilemmas posed by organizational practice.

"When a Lawyer Must Blow the Whistle." Business Week, 21 (May 1979), p. 117.

Reports the submission to the SEC of a petition by the Institute for Public Representation which urged the Commission to promulgate rules relating to corporate counsels' duties toward management, directors, shareholders, and the general public. The regulations would require attorneys to report instances of fraud and unlawful acts to management and the board of directors, or to the SEC, if management failed to act. The author presents views of the Institute, members of the Commission, and attorneys in corporate practice.

G. THE GOVERNMENT LAWYER

De Antonio, Emile, director. Point of Order. Point Films, 1964. 97 min.

This editorial condensation of 188 hours of television kinescopes chronicles the United States Senate's Army-McCarthy Hearings. Senator McCarthy accuses the Army of permitting Communist infiltration of its ranks. The Army countercharges that McCarthy and his chief counsel,

Roy M. Cohn, have used threats to obtain special privileges for Cohn's friend and committee staff investigator G. David Shrine, who had been drafted and sent to Fort Dix.

Frampton, George T, Jr. "Some Practical and Ethical Problems of Prosecuting Public Officials." Maryland Law Review 36 (1976), 5-38.

Discusses significant problems of prosecuting public officials including media leaks, convincing witnesses who may be criminally involved to cooperate, and legal problems relating to pretrial discovery. Ethical issues related to the prosecutorial function that are discussed include the need to build more than customary constitutional safeguards into the investigatory and charging processes, public comments by the prosecutor, plea-bargaining and preparation of government witnesses for trial. Illustrations are provided by reference to the Watergate investigation.

Lowry, Robert P. "Confidences and the Government Lawyer." North Carolina Law Review 57 (1979), 625-646.

Criticizes the Code of Professional Responsibility as couched in terms too broad to be effective in professional practice. The problem of confidentiality in representing a government client is cited to demonstrate this failure.

Marquis, Harold L. "An Appraisal of Attorneys' Responsibilities Before Administrative Agencies." Case West Research Law Review 26 (1976), 285-314.

The Code of Professional Responsibility is formulated for the trial bar and is inadequate as an ethical guide for administrative practice. Administrative proceedings are non-adversary in many cases and involve important public interests. A separate code is required with special rules tailored to particular agencies.

Morrison, Alan B. "Defending the Government: How Vigorous is Too Vigorous?" In Verdicts on Lawyers. Eds. Ralph Nader and Mark Green. New York: Thomas G. Crowell, 1976, pp.242-254.

Discusses the ethical responsibilities of lawyers defending the government. Morrison suggests that such attorneys have a constitutional duty to support and defend the constitution and laws of the United States which transcends his status as an instrument of his government client. Morrison takes issue with the use of delaying tactics and spurious assertions of lack of standing by which government attorneys frustrate public interest litigation against the official or agency they are employed by. Such avoidance tactics burden the federal courts and prevent proper consideration of the attorney's responsibilities to all the people.

Note. "Attorneys: Legal and Professional Ethics: Private Practice and the Former Government Lawyer." Oklahoma Law Review 30 (1977), 365-375.

Discusses ethical considerations that should govern questions of disqualification when attorneys who were formerly employed by government agencies represent, in subsequent private practice, clients before such agencies. Morrison also considers application of Disciplinary Rules that extend disqualification requirements to the attorney's firm.

Note. "Ethical Problems For the Law Firm of a Former Government Attorney: Firm or Individual Disqualification?" Duke Law Journal 1977 (1977), 512-531.

Discusses impact of disqualification requirements of the Code of Professional Resonsibility, where a firm undertakes to represent a client before a government agency which formerly employed a member of the firm. Morrison suggests that in close cases the decision should be made by the court.

Poirier, C. Norman. "Federal Government Lawyer and Professional Ethics." American Bar Association Journal 60 (December 1974), 1541-1544.

Describes supplemental ethical considerations adopted by the Federal Bar Association that apply to civilian attorneys employed in the executive agencies of the federal government. Takes cognizance of inherent limitations placed upon federal attorneys as representatives of the public interest.

Robie, William R. "The Teaching of Professional Responsibility to Federal Government Attorneys: The Uneasy Perceptions." Military Law Review 80 (1978), 29-49.

Discusses Federal Ethical Considerations which implement the Code of Professional Responsibility for members of the Federal Bar Association. Robie surveys courses of training in professional ethics taught to all government employees, including government lawyers who represent government employees, and lawyers who advise federal agencies, attorneys, and structuring plans to meet market demand. Includes first amendment issues, state laws, anti-trust and tax considerations as well as malpractice and fiduciary insurance for attorneys involved in such plans.

Webster, David N. "The Public Defender, the Sixth Amendment, and the Code of Professional Responsibility: The Resolution of a Conflict of Interest." American Criminal Law Review 12 (1975), 739-752.

Examines the applicability of conflict of interest provisions of the Code of Professional Responsibility to public defender attorneys. Webster focuses on the conflict arising when appellate counsel within the office determines that ineffective representation was rendered by trial counsel of the same office. Webster argues that the Sixth Amendment, the Code, and the public interest all require that an attorney recuse himself under such circumstances.

H. LAWYERS AND THE CRIMINAL JUSTICE SYSTEM

Aronson, Robert H. "Toward a Rational Resolution of Ethical Dilemmas in the Criminal Justice System." From Criminal Justice Planning and Development by Alvin W. Cohn. Beverly Hills, CA: Sage, 1977.

Criticizes the Code of Professional Responsibility for failing to provide lawyers in criminal practice with guidance on which of various conflicting duties should take precedence in a particular situation. Aronson argues that in the present system of criminal justice, neither the adversary model nor the truth-oriented model of the attorney's function has been given primacy. Hence large areas of ethical ambiguity persist. He believes the bar should establish a system oriented model and work toward a consensus over the goals of the system. In acting toward these goals individual attorneys would make the ultimate decisions.

Atkins, Burton and Mark Pogrebin, eds. The Invisible Justice System: Discretion and the Law. 2nd ed. Cincinnati, OH: Anderson Publishing Co., 1982.

Includes articles on Discretion and Public Prosecution; Exercising Discretion on the Bench: The Trial Judge's Perspective; Criminal Sentences: Law Without Order; and Discretion and the Determinate Sentence: Its Distribution, Control and Effect on Time Served. A table of cases and index is included.

Bailey, F. Lee. For The Defense. New York: Atheneum, 1975.

Uses anecdotes from his broad courtroom experiences to illustrate inadequacies and inequities in the American system of criminal justice. Bailey recommends restructuring the legal profession so that trial lawyers would fill the roles of defender and prosecutor interchangeably.

Cole, G. F. "American Criminal Lawyer -- A Role Definition." From Administration of Justice System -- An Introduction ed. Donald T. Shanahan. Boston, MA: Holbrook Press, 1977.

Contrasts the proper functions of the defense counsel and prosecutor with their actual roles in an adversary, due process, criminal justice system. Recruitment into criminal practice, financial corporations, interpersonal relations, and the demands for speedy disposition of a huge caseload create needs that are met through a process of administrative practices such as plea bargaining and the decision to charge.

Practicing Law Institute. Advanced Criminal Trial Tactics for Prosecution and Defense. New York: Practicing Law Institute, 1977.

A collection of seminar papers dealing with criminal trial tactics. Discusses problems related to handling informers. Legal and practical problems associated with eyewitness identifications are explored. Discusses effective assertion of a client's Fifth Amendment privileges and current law dealing with electronic surveillance. Another series of papers traces the history of the grand jury and discusses problems related to grand jury investigations.

Schwartz, Murray L. *Cases and Materials on Professional Responsibility and the Administration of Criminal Justice*. New York: Matthew Bender, 1962.

Highlights ethical aspects of the prosecutor's role as a public official. Treats discretion, conduct and responsibility for police practices, the problem of defense counsel in representing a guilty client, the right to counsel and courtroom advocacy.

Sevilla, Charles M. "Between Scylla and Charybdis: The Ethical Perils of the Criminal Defense Lawyer." *National Journal of Criminal Defense* 2 (Fall 1976), 237-285.

Poses hypothetical problems to illustrate areas of defense work which most often present difficult ethical questions. Sevilla suggests solutions to these dilemmas by applying the appropriate rules from the Code of Professional Responsibility and the American Bar Association Standards on the Administration of Criminal Justice.

Weinglass, T. I. "Contempt Problems Facing the Criminal Practitioner." In *Fourteenth Criminal Annual: Defending Criminal Cases*, ed. Ephraim Magolin. Burlingame, CA: San Mateo County Criminal Justice Council, 1976.

Examines cases involving forensic misconduct and analyzes considerations weighed in review of contempt proceedings against attorneys: whether it was an emotional trial for all parties; the state of the attorney's performance throughout the trial; whether the alleged contempt occurred in the course of advocacy or as an aside; and the nature of the language and tone of voice used by counsel.

Wice, Paul. "The Private Practice of Criminal Law: Life in The Real World." *Criminal Law Bulletin* 14 (Sept/Oct. 1978), 381-409.

Describes the day to day practice of private criminal lawyers discussing their personal lives, how they obtain clients, their finances, their relationships with their clients and the ethical problems that beset the practice. Wice notes that criminal lawyers are held in low esteem by corporate attorneys who dominate the organized bar, a group which expends more energy in examining the ethics of the criminal bar than in critical self-examination of its own professional morality.

I. LAWYERS' MORAL CHARACTER

Anderson, Michael, director. The Naked Edge. With Gary Cooper and Deborah Kerr. Pennebaker Inc., 1961. 99 min.

A disbarred attorney attempts to blackmail a successful and extremely wealthy businessman by accusing him of committing the murder of his former employer. The attorney, who actually killed the employer, eventually confesses to the crime.

Bradway, John S. "Moral Turpitude as the Criterion of Offenses That Justify Disbarment." California Law Review 24 (1935), 9-27.

Treats "moral turpitude" as a vague and nebulous expression not clarified by judicial interpretation, which grows out of a criminal background and is inappropriate for professional discipline. Argues that the standard should be particularly applicable to professional conduct, should include professional and private conduct, should be appropriate to disciplinary rather than penal proceedings and should be flexible and discretionary. The standard should be embodied in a professional code.

Comment. "The Concept of Attorney-Fitness in New York: New Perspectives." Buffalo Law Review 24 (1975), 553-566.

Discusses In re Kimball 33 New York 2d 586, 301 N.E. 2d 436 (1973), a New York case involving the application for admission to the bar of an attorney who had previously been disbarred in Florida after a sodomy conviction. Author argues that this case portends less reliance on irrelevant prior convictions and disciplinary proceedings in determining fitness for admission to the bar.

Comment. "Florida Bar Admission Rule Requiring Good Moral Character Does Not Defeat the Purpose of the Federal Bankruptcy Act in Violation of the Supremacy Clause of the United States Constitution." Florida State University Law Review 7 (1979), 587-592.

Discusses two Florida cases involving applicants for admission to the state bar who availed themselves of federal personal bankruptcy law in attempts to avoid repaying student loans and other debts. The bar association found that they had acted in bad faith and did not exhibit good moral character. Florida Supreme Court held that such denial does not interfere with federal policy embodied in the Bankruptcy Act, which is to give debtors a fresh start after a bankruptcy. The Court said that its decision did not result in discrimination based solely upon the petitioners' status as bankrupts, but based upon collateral aspects of their activities that were indicative of bad character.

Comment. "Good Moral Character and Admission to the Bar." <u>Cincinnatti University Law Review</u> 48 (1979), 876-885.

Discusses two Florida cases involving challenges to individuals' admission to the bar because of bad faith filing in bankruptcy to avoid payment of educational loans. Both cases were factually similar, but one person was denied admission while the other was admitted. The author argues that the only distinction between the two cases is that one petitioner was divorced and had two children while the other was unmarried. The unmarried one was denied admission. Author finds this illustrative of the arbitrariness of a good moral character standard which, in effect, allows case by case determination of fitness based on a vague and arbitary standard.

Comment. "Good Moral Character and Homosexuality." <u>Journal of the Legal Profession</u> 5 (1980), 139-149.

Discusses instances of disbarment or denial of admission to practice law because of poor moral character, specifically homosexuality. The author concludes that while it may be an aspect of poor moral character in some instances, the behavior involved must be inimical to the goals served by the good moral character requirement.

Comment. "The Good Moral Character Requirement for Admission to the Bar." <u>University of San Fernando Valley Law Review</u> 4 (1975), 317-331.

Discusses the history of bar admission character requirements in California. Evidence of moral turpitude, as a basis for denial of admission disbarment, is criticized since it is not clear what such evidence should constitute. Author disputes the wisdom of imposing a requirement that candidates conform to a single moral standard as an arbitrary imposition of values.

Comment. "Homosexuality and the Good Moral Character Requirement." University of Detroit Journal of Urban Law 56 (1978), 123-139.

Discusses the good moral character requirement generally, and specifically with relation to extra- professional conduct. Also discusses the legal status of homosexuality and its impact on members of the Bar. Concludes that private consensual acts do not impinge upon interests of the bar, the courts, or the public.*

Carothers, Graham C. "Character and Fitness: A Need for Increased Perception." The Bar Examiner 51:3 (August 1982), 25-34.

Focuses on questions and problems which arise in cases brought to bar examiners for prosecution and deliberation. Carothers considers the problem and factors inherent in the character and fitness decision making process. He assesses the need for attorneys to be of 'good moral character'. He studies the kind of conduct for which practicing attorneys can be disciplined as a means of identifying character traits important in the initial character and fitness investigation. Finally, he examines the roles of bar examiners and courts.

Custer, Lawerence B. "Georgia's Board to Determine Fitness of Bar Applicants". The Bar Examiner pp. 17-21.

Outlines the reasons for the establishment of the Georgia Board to determine Fitness of Bar Applicants. Describes procedures and guidelines used in approving or denying applications and the effect the existence of the board has on the application process. Custer, its current chairman, claims that no other Georgia institution is doing as much for the improvement of the bar and the protection of the public.

Delaney, Hubert T. "The Lawyers' Right to Exercise the Privileges of Citizenship." Lawyers Guild Review 13 (1953), 26-28.

Describes the nature of attacks against lawyers during the McCarthy period, including the imposition of loyalty oaths, 1952 proposals to disbar lawyers who were members of the Communist Party or who advocated Marxism-Leninism, and the 1953 proposals to punish lawyers for their "attitude" before nonjudicial branches of government.

Elliston, Frederick A. "Character and Fitness Tests: An Ethical Perspective." The Bar Examiner 51:3 (August 1982) pp. 8-16.

Examines character and fitness tests from "the moral point of view." Elliston poses theoretical and factual challenges to current policy which applies community standards of morality and character to those who seek to practice law. He considers the purpose of fitness tests an proposes an alternative. Finally, he suggests an abandonment by Fitness Boards of the rehabilitation ideology in favor of an ideology of just desserts.

Eshete, Andreas. "Does a Lawyer's Character Matter?." From The Good Lawyer ed. David Luban. Totowa, NJ: Rowman & Allanheld, 1984, pp. 270-285.

Indicates how lawyers fall into morally compromising positions. Eshete describes how and what lawyers are asked to do, the training that prepares them the conception governing their profession and the problems they meet draw them into dubious conduct. He suggests that recognizing the forces that make lawyers susceptible to morally suspect attitudes and actions does not remove all our worries. Finally, he identifies legal situations in which lawyers cannot justifiably engage in squalid conduct. where lawyers directly encounter issues that arise in other areas of public life their resolution calls for personal virtues. If lawyers were guided by a conception of their role suited to these settings, they might avoid dangers now attending their work.

Herman, James E. "Screening for Character and Fitness." Bar Examiner 51 (1982), 23-25.

Florida Supreme Court has final constitutional jurisdiction over admission to the bar. The Board of Law Examiners interviews applicant, who must produce evidence of good moral character. One lacks such character if there is evidence of acts and conduct which would cause a reasonable man to have doubts about an individual's honesty, fairness, and respect for rights of others and for law (citing Florida Board of Law Examiners, 364 So. 2d

454, 458 (1978). Due process requires that there be a reasonable relationship between requirements for admission and an applicant's fitness to practice law.

Hill, Harold N. Jr. "Appellate Review of Moral Character and Fitness Determinations". The Bar Examiner 51:3 (August 1982) pp. 22-24.

The Presiding Justice of the Supreme Court of Georgia raises questions about the proper role of Appellate Courts in granting or denying admission to the bar, and the correct standards for Appellate review of character and fitness determinations. Hill argues there is presently no better solution to the problem of determining the moral character and fitness of those admitted to the bar than character fitness investigations and appeals.

Kaslow, Florence W. "Moral, Emotional and Physical fitness for the Bar: Pondering (seeming) Imponderables". The Bar Examiner 51:3 (August 1982) pp. 38-48.

A mental health professional asks who defines moral fitness and mental responsibility. She speculates about the Kohlberg-level of moral development one must attain in order to be morally fit to practice law. Emotional and physical fitness issues are discussed with several cases alluded to in which pertinent arguments regarding criteria for fitness determinations are presented.

Schwartz, Arthur H. "What is a Character and Fitness Committee?" New York State Bar Journal 49 (1977), 302-306, 398-401, 440-442, 494-499.

Discusses procedure of New York State committees and leading Supreme Court and New York cases.

Starrs, John R. "Considerations in Determination of Good Moral Character." Catholic Lawyer 2 (1956), 161-171.

Discusses various attempts by judges and philosophers to formulate standards of good moral character. Starrs concludes that the general principles of Judeo-Christian morality must be the general rules by which an applicant for admission to the bar must live if he is to be considered of good moral character.

Weckstein, Donald T. "Maintaining The Integrity and Competence of the Legal Profession." Texas Law Review 48 (1970), 267-284.

Critique of Canon One of the Code of Professional Responsibility. Weckstein comments on moral character requirements and the responsibility of the attorney to cooperate with authorities in enforcing the Code.

CHAPTER FOUR
LAW AS A BUSINESS

A. ADVERTISING IN LAW

Branca, John G., and Marc I. Steinberg. "Attorney Fee Schedules and Legal Advertising - Implications of Goldfarb." University of California Los Angeles Law Review 24:3 (1977), 475-522.

Addresses fee-setting schedules and attorney advertising in the light of the U.S. Supreme Court's holding in Goldfarb v. Virginia State Bar. Considers applicability of anti-trust law in cases of fee schedules and offers alternatives that may not run afoul of that law. These include a relative value scale for attorney services based on the nature of the service provided and dissemination of information by the bar about attorneys' fees in the locality that would enable both attorneys and the public to determine whether fees are competitive.

Christensen, Harold G. "Advertising by Lawyers." Utah Law Review 1978 (1978), 619-634.

Discusses the historical development of bar rules forbidding or limiting lawyer advertising, the effects of consumerism on their underlying rationale and recent case law developments. Christensen favors truthful advertising of routine legal services but would prohibit solicitation which he distinguishes from advertising.

Comment. "Bates v. State Bar of Arizona: A Consumers' Rights Interpretation of the First Amendment Ends Bans on Legal Advertising." Denver Law Journal 55 (1978), 103-129.

In Bates v. State Bar of Arizona, the Supreme Court held that a blanket suppression of legal advertising violates the First Amendment guarantee of freedom of speech. The author hails the decision as a triumph of consumerism, ensuring the free flow of information in the market place so that consumers may make informed decisions when seeking legal services.

Figa, Phillip S. "Lawyer Solicitation Today and Under the Proposed Model Rules of Professional Conduct." *University of Colorado Law Review* 52 (1981), 393-408.

Compares the restrictions in advertising and solicitation embodied in the Code of Professional Responsibility, judicial decisions that have opened up new fields of activity in these areas, and the provisions of the Model Rules of Professional Conduct.

Francis, Paul and Jennifer Johnson. "The Emperor's Old Clothes: Piercing the Bar's Ethical Veil." *Willamette Law Journal* 13 (1977), 221-271.

Discusses the probable application of the anti-trust laws to the legal profession, arguing that the ethical concerns long raised by the bar against attorney advertising have become obsolete and no longer serve the public or the profession.

Hinchey, John W. "The First Amendment and the Delivery of Legal Services." *American Bar Asociation Journal* 63 (1977), 945-950.

Argues that advertising by lawyers is commercial speech protected by the First Amendment. Hinchey notes that the Amendment does not protect false or deceptive commercial speech nor may it be used to stir up litigation. He argues these recognized constitutional limits and the public interest in the availability of legal services permit non-deceptive advertising by lawyers.

"Is Advertising Laying an Egg? Lawyers May be More Interested in Solicitation." *American Bar Asociation Journal* 64 (May 1978), 673-674.

American Bar Asociation Law Poll found the majority of attorneys and law firms are disinclined to advertise. The poll showed that though most attorneys oppose allowing solicitation, more attorneys would use solicitation than advertising if it were permitted.

Jeffers, Leroy. "Institute on Advertising Within the Legal Profession." *Oklahoma Law Review* 29 (1976), 620-628.

Argues against advertising by lawyers because competition for clients is an activity inconsistent with the character and function of the profession. Jeffers fears this would lead to de-professionalization and ensuing loss of autonomy.

Morrison, Alan B. "Institute an Advertising Within the Legal Profession - Pro." Oklahoma Law Review 29 (1976), 609-619.

Discusses general arguments for relaxing restrictions on advertising. Morrison notes that advertising would benefit consumers in need of legal services and that there are serious questions as to whether bar imposed restrictions constitute violations of the anti-trust law and the First Amendment.

Smith, Cullen. "Reflections On the Ethical Development of Prepaid Legal Services." Baylor Law Review 27 (1975), 427-430.

Introduces a symposium on prepaid legal services. Smith discusses factors which led to the adoption of amendments to the Code of Professional Responsibility that would remove restrictions on advertising, solicitation and the development of prepaid legal services: court challenges to bar association restrictions on advertising, cost of legal services and consumer group agitation for change. The symposium contains articles on tax and anti-trust aspects of prepaid legal services.

"To Advertise Or Not To Advertise." American Bar Asociation Journal 63 (1977), 341-345.

Discusses the Supreme Court case of Bates v. State Bar of Arizona in which advertising of legal services by attorneys was at issue. The article includes a summary of the parties' briefs and questions, with counsels' response to them.

Note. "Advertising, Solicitation and the Professional's Duty to Make Legal Counsel Available." Yale Law Journal 81 (1972), 1181-1208.

Believes bar-imposed limitations on advertising and solicitation are unconstitutional. The author argues that properly regulated, these practices will educate people about their legal rights and foster economic changes in the delivery of legal services that will bring them within the reach of more consumers.

Note. "Attorneys: New Developments in Lawyer Advertising - Will the New Oklahoma Plan Pass Constitutional Muster?" Oklahoma Law Review 30 (1977), 376-385.

Discusses recent amendments to the Oklahoma Code of Professional Ethics which permit attorneys to advertise their fees, specialties and services. The author also discusses constitutional issues involved in the regulation of lawyers' advertising (First Amendment) and antitrust questions raised by bar association regulation of fees.

B. THE DISTRIBUTION OF LEGAL SERVICES

Abel, Richard I. "Socializing the Legal Profession: Can Re-Distributing Lawyers' Services Achieve Social Justice?" Law and Policy Quarterly 1:1 (January 1979), 5-51.

Examines reforms to redistribute lawyers' services. Generally they attempt to modify the market distribution in one of two ways: by subsidizing lawyers for the otherwise unrepresented; or by rendering lawyers unnecessary through deprofessionalization. Abel appraises the contribution to social justice under the greatest conceivable redistribution: a socialization of the profession that would withdraw lawyers from those who presently employ lawyers' services, while simultaneously subsidizing lawyers for the unrepresented.

Abel, Richard L. "Toward a Political Economy of Lawyers." Wisconsin Law Review 1981 (1981), 1117-1187.

Using data gathered by a British Commission on legal services, Abel attempts to develop a sociology of the legal profession. His analysis begins with the axiom that all occupations under capitalism seek market control, the attainment of which is the defining characteristic of a profession. The legal profession was earlier successful, but its market control has since eroded. Its response has been to stimulate demand and to defend and recapture control. Changes in the structures within which legal services are produced have resulted in new efforts to legitimate control of the market. These legitimations have had significant impact upon professional behavior. Abel concludes that the profession as an economic, social, and political institution is moribund.

"Antitrust and Ethical Aspects of Lawyers' Minimum Fee Schedules." *Real Property Probate and Trust Journal* 7:4 (1972), 726-739.

Discussion of property and probate aspects of bar attempts to regulate fees. Broadened concepts of interstate commerce lead to conflicts between state bar association attempts to regulate and federal anti-trust laws. The bar may not be so closely identified with the state to exempt its actions from federal anti-trust legislation. A major concern for reform in this area is to make legal services more generally available.

Armstrong, Walter P. "Ethical Problems in Connection With the Delivery of Legal Services." *San Diego Law Review* 12 (1975), 336-358.

Describes bar efforts to implement the profession's obligation to make legal services more widely available by amending provisions of the Code of Professional Responsibility. The Code has been severely criticized for discouraging the development of legal aid agencies, clinics and group legal services.

Bayles, Michael D. "A Problem of Clean Hands: Refusal to Provide Professional Services." *Social Theory and Practice*, 5:2 (Spring 1979), 165-181. Reprinted in *Ethics and the Legal Profession* eds. Frederick A. Elliston and Michael Davis. Buffalo, NY: Prometheus, 1984.

Considers the claim that a professional who refuses to provide services on ethical grounds should refer the client to a professional who will provide them. Bayles argues that this claim rests upon a confusion between moral and personal norms and that by such referrals the professional aids the commission of moral wrong. He then considers the claim that the professional has good ethical reasons to provide the service even though the prospective client will receive them elsewhere. Finally, he argues against the claim that if no other professional is available, it is more difficult to justify refusal. Bayles claims instead that only in such cases does a professional have a good moral reason for refusal.

Bodle, George E. "Group Legal Services: the Case for *BRT*." *University of California Los Angeles Law Review* 12 (1965), 306-326.

Discusses the case of *BRT v. Virginia State Bar* in which the U.S. Supreme Court held bar restrictions on group legal services plans violate the First Amendment. Bodle believes the decision should provide an impetus for change in the ways in which the profession has made its services available to the public in the past.

Brownell, Emery A. *Legal Aid in the United States*. Rochester, NY: Lawyers Cooperative Publishing Co., 1951.

A study of the availability of lawyers' services for persons unable to pay fees. Brownell's attitude and description are imbued with a paternalistic tinge.

Christensen, Barlow F. "Toward Improved Legal Service Delivery: A Look at Four Mechanisms." *American Bar Foundation Research Journal* 2 (1979), 277-293.

Evaluates lawyer advertising, specialty certification, lawyer directory, and lawyer referral mechanisms with respect to their performance in diagnosing legal problems, providing information needed for an informed selection of a lawyer and aiding prospective clients in making the initial contact. Systems combining directory and referral mechanisms are judged the best possible approaches.

Comment. "Group Legal Services, The Ethical Evolution." *Baylor Law Review* 27 (1975), 525-543.

Describes public demand for group legal services and the effects of amendments to the Code of Professional Responsibility intended to make this possible. The impetus for reform is largely the result of Supreme Court decisions in cases involving non-profit organizations that provided, as an ancillary service, legal representation for financial benefit (NAACP v. Button; Brotherhood of Railroad Trainmen v. Virginia State Bar; United Mine Workers v. Illinois State Bar Association).

Comment. "Legal Services - Past and Present." *Cornell Law Review* 59 (1974), 960-988.

Describes the development of the Legal Services Program (LSP) of the Office of Economic Opportunity and its achievements in setting up regional offices, influencing developments in poverty law, generating research and cultivating cooperation with the organized bar. The author notes that controversy has arisen concerning the ethical propriety of some LSP activities. Working for them poses the possibility of interference with the lawyer's independent judgment in advising a client. This controversy is likely to persist with the replacement of the LSP by the National Legal Services Corporation.

Comment. "The Shreveport and Columbus Plans of Prepaid Legal Services - An Analysis of Plans Presently in Operation." Baylor Law Review 27 (1975), 485-499.

Describes two urban examples of prepaid legal services. The author believes that such plans tend to attract a membership that is socioeconomically homogeneous, a factor that must be considered in designing a plan.

Curran, Barbara A. The Legal Needs of the Public: The Final Report of a National Survey. Chicago, IL: American Bar Foundation, 1977.

Reports the results of a comprehensive survey on legal needs jointly undertaken by the American Bar Foundation and the American Bar Association's Special Committee to Survey the Legal Needs of the Public. Curan explores the extent of legal problems, ways legal services are used, kinds of lawyers sought and method of selection, the public's reaction to legal costs, and attitudes toward lawyers and the legal system. A research bibliography and survey instruments are appended.

Francis, Paul H., "Legal Aid: The Demise of Idealism." Wayne State Law Review 23 (1977), 1261-1292.

Details the history of the National Legal Services Corporation and its controversial predecessor, the Office of Economic Opportunity's Legal Services program. Francis discusses challenges levelled against the Legal Services Program on the grounds that it interfered with attorney-client relationships. He describes resistance to the program's activities by state governments and attempts by Congress to curb those activities. He discusses problems to be faced by the corporation--especially the strong law-reform orientation of its employees and affiliates.

Galanter, Marc. "The Duty Not To Deliver Legal Services." University of Miami Law Review 30 (1976), 929-951.

The market system of supplying legal services is inadequate. Galanter suggests that new forms of dispute resolution and augmented legal services may replace the delivery of traditional lawyers' services as the responsibility of the profession.

Huber, Stephen K. "Competition at the Bar and the Proposed Code of Professional Standards." North Carolina Law Review 57 (1979), 559-596.

Argues that the rapid obsolescence of the 1969 Code of Professional Responsibility arose because it did not permit the delivery of legal services to be organized in an efficient and cost-minimizing manner. Huber discusses competitive pricing, advertising, solicitation and the manner in which the Code has interfered with them as a means of making legal services generally available.

Hunter, Robert S. "Slave Labor in the Courts: A Suggested Solution." Case and Comment 74 (1969), 3-12.

Argues that attorneys will do a better job for the poor if they are paid more and shows a state-by-state breakdown of attorney compensation.

Kettleson, Jeanne. "Ethical Outlook - Revising the Code of Professional Responsibility." NLADA Briefcase 35 (Mar. 1978), 40-43.

Discusses the problem posed to the staff of a legal service program when they must choose between turning people away who need help or providing less than adequate service to all who apply. The Code of Professional Responsibility does not appear to permit the latter of these two choices and Ketttleson concludes that it is not an effective way of dealing with the problems of limited resources.

Marks, F. Raymond. "A Lawyer's Duty to Take All Comers and Many Who Do Not Come." University of Miami Law Review 30 (1976), 915-927.

Discusses the legal profession's failure to meet the needs of low income groups. Marks argues that lawyers have a duty to make these services available to all who need them which goes beyond the requirements of the Code of Professional Responsibility. He suggests reforms that would improve the present system of delivering legal services, including tax incentives and ultimately a full socialization of legal services.

Nader, Ralph, and Mark Green. Verdicts on Lawyers. New York: Thomas Y. Crowell, 1976.

Examines the dual functions of the organized bar as a self-disciplinary and self-interested regulatory agency; the ethical effects of this dual role; judicial selection; availability of legal services; and the cost of such services. Contains sections on corporate and government practice and on the role and quality of judges and considers the possibility of federal regulation of the bar.

Nahstoll, R.W. "Limitations on Group Legal Services Arrangements Under the Code of Professional Responsibility, D.R. 2-103 (D)(5): Stale Wine in New Bottles." Texas Law Review 48 (Jan. 1970), 334-350.

Castigates the draftsmen of the Code for failure to enact disciplinary rules that extend rather than detract and disserve the ethical considerations with respect to development of group legal services. Nahstoll proposes an alternative disciplinary rule governing such arrangements.

National Resource Center for Consumers of Legal Services. Group Legal Service Plans: Organization, Operation and Management. New York: Law & Business, 1981.

Describes in detail the organization, operation and management of prepaid group legal service plans. Discusses the impact that this development is likely to have on society, the courts and the profession. Various plans are presented as well as the means of marketing them, selecting attorneys and structuring plans to meet market demand. Includes First Amendment issues, state laws, anti-trust and tax considerations as well as malpractice and fiduciary insurance for attorneys involved in such plans.

Oberiek, Hans. "Clean Hands and Professional Responsibility: A Rejoinder to Michael Bayles." Moral Responsibility and the Professions eds. Bernard Baumrin and Benjamin Freedman. New York: Haven Publications, 1983, pp. 151-155.

Defends the "standard view" that a professional has good reason to refuse a client who proposes to perform immoral conduct, but may refer him to someone else who will provide the services. Part one offers a utilitarian defense. Part two criticizes Bayles's argument with its appeal to consequentialism. Part three contends that Bayles's position would make a mockery out of our moral life if generalized.

Schwartz, Murray L. "Foreword: Group Legal Services in Perspective." University of California Los Angeles Law Review 12 (1965), 279-305.

Discusses Brotherhood of Railroad Trainmen v. Virginia State Bar in which the U.S. Supreme Court held rules of the Virginia State Bar Association that forbade group legal services plans in violation of the First Amendment. Schwartz believes the profession should make legal services more generally available in light of this decision.

Simpson, Frank. "Group Legal Services: The Case For Caution." University of California Los Angeles Law Review 12 (1965), 327-340.

Argues that U.S. Supreme Court cases purporting to lift restrictions on the development of group legal services have been interpeted too broadly by advocates of group services. Simpson finds no adequate public policy reasons to justify changes that threaten to transform legal practice from a profession to a commercial enterprise and no substantial need for group legal services.

Smith, Chesterfield H. "A Mandatory Pro Bono Service Standard - Its Time Has Come." University of Miami Law Review 35 (1981), 727-737.

Proposes a definitive, but flexible, pro bono rule to govern lawyers' conduct. The flexible nature of such a rule would accommodate lawyers' individual circumstances while serving the needs of society.

Smith, Eugene T. "Canon 2: A Lawyer Should Assist The Legal Profession In Fulfilling Its Duty to Make Legal Counsel Available." Texas Law Review 48 (1970), 285-310.

Criticizes Canon 2 of the Code of Professional Responsibility which deals with advertising and solicitation because it does not adequately deal with group legal services.

Staton, Robert H. "Access to Legal Services Through Advertising and Specialization." *Indiana Law Journal* 53 (1977-78), 247-276.

Discusses advertising guidelines adopted by the Indiana Supreme Court in the wake of Supreme Court decisions opening up the field of advertising services, fees and specialties by lawyers. Appendices include a copy of the applicable disciplinary rules and the report of the Lawyer Advertising Committee of the Indiana State Bar Association.

Stewart, Potter. "Professional Ethics for the Business Lawyer - Morals of the Market Place." *Business Lawyer* 31:1 (1975), 463-468.

Discusses the Supreme Court's decision in *Goldfarb v. Virginia State Bar* in which county and state bar minimum fee schedules restrained trade. Supreme Court Justice Stewart argues that the public is best served by competition among lawyers and that the ethics of the business lawyer should be no more than the morals of the market place. The business lawyer should zealously represent his client. Other ethical considerations are matters for an individual's conscience.

Stone, Alan A. "Legal Education in the Couch." *Harvard Law Review* 85 (1971), 392-441.

Survey of psychological dimensions of conflict in values between activist law students and faculty. Stone analyzes student criticisms concluding that, though excessively broad, it does suggest substantial reform is needed. He discusses psychological implications of adopting clinical legal education as a major reform.

Weckstein, Donald T. "Limitations On the Right To Counsel: The Unauthorized Practice of Law." *Utah Law Review* 1978 (1978), 649-680.

Examines the goals of unauthorized practice restrictions, analyzes their scope, evaluates their application in various contexts and proposes a framework for future resolution of issues. Weckstein discusses antitrust and constitutional issues raised against unauthorized practice restrictions. He proposes that litigants in non-criminal cases be allowed to choose to be assisted by a non-lawyer who can demonstrate qualifications sufficient to handle the matter.

Wise, Raymond L. Legal Ethics. New York: Matthew Bender, 1966.

Applies the Canons of Professional Ethics to the practice of law. Contains sections on building a practice, advertising, law lists, counsel work, separate occupations, partnerships, intermediaries, fees, conflicts of interest, privileges, client relations and advocacy.

Wolfram, Charles. "A Lawyer's Duty to Represent Clients, Repugnant and Otherwise." From The Good Lawyer ed. David Luban. Totowa, NJ: Rowman & Allanheld, 1984, pp. 214-235.

Addresses the issue of whether, once a decision to represent a client has been made, the lawyer may be tarred with the same brush as the client. Wolfram reviews the "professional" regulations that lawyers have drafted for themselves. According to them no duty exists to represent a client except when a court or bar association appoints a lawyer. He explores the dimensions of a moral duty to accept a client. Finally, Wolfram confronts the specialized problem of repugnant but necessitous clients whom lawyers of normal moral sensitivity personally feel compelled to represent.

Zander, Michael. "How to Explain the Unmet Need for Legal Services?" American Bar Association Journal 64 (Nov. 1978), 1676-79.

A 1977 study by the American Bar Association and the American Bar Foundation indicated that lawyers were consulted in slightly less than one third of all legal matters. Three theories are analyzed to explain this: the poverty theory; the legal incompetence theory; and the social organization theory. The most significant difference between those who take legal advice and those who do not may be the fact that one group has contact with a knowledgeable lay intermediary while the other does not.

C. REGULATION AND DISCIPLINE

Akers, Ronald L. "The Professional Asociation and the Legal Regulation of Practice." Law and Society Review 2 (1968), 413-482.

Draws from research on the professional associations of several health professions. Akers discusses their activities in influencing legislation. He describes patterns of organization, the interrelationship and rivalryamong them, as well as their public relations activities.

Albert, Edward. "How 42 Lawyers Were Disbarred in New York - as an Indirect Result of the Grisly David Berkowitz Murder Case." Barrister 7 (Summer 1980), 6-8.

Describes the antics of a sometime counsel for the defendant in a notorious murder case. Though convicted of a felony, the attorney emphasizes he was not disbarred. He discusses New York case law on the use of prior convictions in attorney disciplinary proceedings.

American Bar Association. Consortium For Professional Education. "Preventing Legal Malpractice." Videotapes (4 tapes, 2 hours), 1978.

Each videotape includes a dramatization followed by a brief panel discussion of typical problems and pitfalls faced by practicing attorneys. Topics include incidents that often give rise to liability; measures to prevent neglect and oversight; developments in the law that have increased lawyers' vulnerability; case law in areas central to malpractice - conflict and disclosure, competence and specialization; and standard of care.

American Bar Association. National Center For Professional Responsibility. The Rules File. Chicago: American Bar Association, 1981. (microfiche cards).

A collection of rules for every state jurisdiction pertaining to disciplinary enforcement, clients' security funds, ethical codes and fee arbitation.

American Bar Foundation. Unauthorized Practice Source Book. Rev. ed. Chicago: American Bar Foundation, 1965.

A collection of source materials dealing with aspects of unauthorized practice, its impact upon the public and the profession, and ways to prevent it. Materials listed include books, articles, judicial decisions and ethics opinions by bar association ethics committees. The unauthorized practice of law is distinguished from the professional practice of law and sources are listed for treating numerous activities that encroach on the authorized practice of law such as collection agencies, realtors' services, services by other professionals, estate planners and tax advisors.

Annunziato, Edward S. "Access To the Work Product of an Attorney Disqualified For Opposing a Former Client: First Wisconsin Mortgage Trust." Vanderbilt Law Review 32 (1979), 819-833.

Discusses First Wisconsin Mortgage Trust v. First Wisconsin Corp., which addressed disqualification of an attorney for opposing a former client and established a test for determining when the disqualified attorney's work product could be passed on to the succeeding attorney without violating the Code of Professional Responsibility. The court's decision should turn upon whether the work product was generated at a time when the attorney could have been influenced by his former client's confidences and whether it was a product of the attorney's judgment, impressions or strategy. If the court finds both of these conditions to exist, then access should be denied.

Arkin, Stanley S. "Self-Regulation and Approaches to Maintaining Standards of Professional Integrity." University of Miami Law Review 30 (1976), 803-846.

Examines self-regulation by utilizing the lawyer disciplinary process in a New York City judicial district. Arkin describes the procedures, discusses objections to self-regulation from bar and lay viewpoints and suggests reforms to allay public dissatisfaction with the profession.

Aronson, Robert H. Attorney-Client Fee Arrangements: Regulation and Review. Washington, DC: The Federal Judicial Center, 1980.

Reports on a study undertaken by the Federal Judicial Center. Discusses valuation of legal services, fee splitting, contingent fee arrangements and funding of public interest litigation through awarding of attorneys' fees. Numerous case references are included and the appendix lists Federal fee award statutes.

Bagg, Deborah A. "What the Devitt Committee Recommends to Improve Advocacy in Federal Courts." Judicature 63:7 (Feb. 1980), 309-321.

The Devitt Committee reported that over 25 percent of the performances by lawyers in cases that come to trial in federal district courts were rated as less than 'good' by the presiding judge; that 41.3 percent of the judges answering a questionnaire believed there is a serious problem of inadequate trial advocacy in their courts; that trial lawyers who answered the lawyers' opinion questionnaires concluded similarly; and that general legal knowledge and skills in examining witnesses and planning and managing litigation needed improvement. The committee's final recommendations for individual district action included a bar exam as a condition for admission to practice, a requirement of four supervised trial experiences, peer review, institution of the first three recommendations in pilot districts, adoption of a student practice rule, and continuing legal education. A list of the committee members are provided, as well as guidelines suggested by the judicial conference.

Carpenter, Edmund N. "Negligent Attorney Embezzler: Delaware's Solution." American Bar Association Journal 61 (1975), 338-341.

Describes the Delaware Bar Association's response to the problem of attorney's who commingle their funds with those of their clients and subsequently misappropriate their clients' money. The association created a special disciplinary committee and established stringent disclosures and bookkeeping requirements regarding attorneys' bank accounts. The committee is also empowered to make spot inspections of books and accounts.

Cavanagh, Randolph C. and Deborah L. Rhode. "The Unauthorized Practice of Law and Pro Se Divorce: An Empirical Analysis." Yale Law Journal 86 (1976), 103-184.

Evaluates the justifications for invoking unauthorized practice prohibitions in the context of pro se divorce. The authors review the arguments against the use of "divorce-yourself kits" and the results of 331 uncontested divorce files. Their purpose was to identify discrete functions performed by lawyers in uncontested divorce actions. They conclude that the data does not support the continuation of a lawyer-monopoly over uncontested divorces.

Cheek, James H. "Professional Responsibility and Self-Regulation of the Securities Lawyer." Washington and Lee Law Review 32 (1975), 597-636.

Discusses the difficulties posed by the lack of clear guidance for attorneys involved in securities regulation about their obligations toward the public. Cheek notes a trend toward expanded liability and believes the bar must take the initiative in developing standards of professional responsibility before the courts do.

Christensen, Barlow F. "Lawyer Referral Service: An Alternative to Lay-Group Legal Services?" University of California Los Angeles Law Review 12 (1965), 341-350.

Describes the lawyer referral service of the American Bar Association in theory and in practice, testing it as an alternative to legal service plans operated by lay groups.

Comment. "Controlling Lawyers by Bar Associations and Courts." Harvard Civil Rights and Civil Liberty Law Review 5 (1970), 301-392.

Notes incidents of alleged judicial and bar association moves to harass and discipline lawyers representing unpopular clients who engage in social activism. The author discusses the historical development of the ethical precepts on which these disciplinary actions have been founded. The terms moral turpitude, misconduct, solicitation and advertising as used in this context are defined and First Amendment rights, the right to advertise legal services and the use of judicial contempt power to control attorneys in court are discussed.

Comment. "Discipline of Attorneys for Non-Professional Misconduct." Arkansas Law Review 5 (1951), 411-419.

General discussion of case law regarding the discipline of attorneys for non-professional misconduct. The author takes issue with cases that tend to impose too strict a standard of morality upon attorneys and argues that to justify disbarment the offense should be relevant to the criteria of conduct appropriate for a good lawyer.

Comment. "Professional Ethics and Trial Publicity: Another Constitutional Attack on DR7-107 Hirschkop v. Snead." University of Richmond Law Review 14 (1979), 213-249.

In Hirschkop v. Snead an attorney sought an injunction against DR7-107, forbidding extra-judicial comments by attorneys on pending litigation with which they were associated. The Court held that the prohibition applied only to criminal cases tried before a jury. The rule also purports to govern attorneys' comments in other proceedings, but the court found those prohibitions void because they were to broad. The author argues that the case does not provide a clear standard to govern extra-judicial statements by lawyers, nor does it point out a compelling government interest in restricting attorneys' First Amendment rights.

Cox, Archibald. "The Lawyer's Independent Calling." Kentucky Law Journal 67:1 (1979/1979), 5-26.

Celebrates the varied roles of attorneys in American society. Cox advocates a voluntary assumption by individual attorneys of high personal moral standards that must be expressed in their dealings with clients. A spirit of independence, he feels, is essential to the effectiveness of the lawyer and the profession.

Dreibelbis, Ellen. "Ain't Misbehavin'." California State Bar Journal 55 (July 1980), 304-306.

Contains advice and addresses for practicing attorneys who seek state bar association opinions on ethical problems.

Garbus, Martin and J. Seligman. "Sanctions and Disbarment: They Sit in Judgment." In Verdicts on Lawyers. eds. Ralph Nader and Mark Green. New York: Thomas Y. Crowell, 1976.

Points out that only a small fraction of violations of ethical norms are even processed by the bar's disciplinary machinery. Disciplinary agencies have little power or neglect to proceed against prominent firms or attorneys. The bar's ethical standards are not supported by an effective disciplinary mechanism. The authors recommend more funding and citizen participation.

Hall, Thomas J. and Joel C. Levy. "Intra-Attorney Fee Sharing Arrangements." Valparaiso University Law Review 11 (1976), 1-28.

Analyzes the ethical and legal considerations applicable to fee sharing arrangements and suggests standards for contracting and enforcing such agreements. The authors trace the development of current standards for fee sharing and conclude that the greatest aid to avoiding disputes is not the refusal to answer questions concerning political affiliations and opinions.

Kaplan, Stanley A. "Professional Competence: How To Measure It, What To Do About It." American Bar Association Journal 63 (1977), 1645-1649.

Presents arguments for and against liability in malpractice and discusses clause 6 of the code of Professional Responsibility (requiring competence with respect to a client's affairs) in a hypothetical relationship between malpractice and professional responsibility under the code.

Kidney, James. "Lawyers -- Can They Police Themselves?" From Readings in Criminal Justice 1978, 1979 annual editions by Donald E.J. MacNamara. Guilford, CT: Dushkin Publishing Group, Inc., 1978.

Evidence that the legal profession is increasing its efforts to rid itself of dishonest and incompetent practitioners is cited. The drive to upgrade the profession is being undertaken in the hopes of restoring public confidence in the bar after the publicity surrounding Watergate and the criminal activities of lawyers holding positions of public trust. Many state bar associations are responding to complaints that lawyers have either stolen money from their clients or neglected their duties in court. Aspects of the campaign to improve the legal profession are discussed, with quotes from bar association officials and others. Disciplinary sanctions for errant lawyers are noted, and guidelines for avoiding problems when hiring an attorney are presented.

Liebman, Howard M. "The Changing Law of Disqualification: The Role of Presumption and Policy." North West University Law Review 73 (1979), 996-1037.

Examines leading cases involving attorney disqualification. Liebman discusses ethical and practical considerations. He believes that law firms have very little guidance in making the decision to disqualify.

Lobato, Ebar, director. <u>Scream of The Butterfly</u>. With Nelida Lobato and Nick Novarro. Emerson Film Enterprises, 1965. 76 min.

A young man is arrested for the savage murder of his lover, but to the consternation of the assistant district attorney in charge of the case, the district attorney seems strangely reluctant to prosecute, preferring to commit the murderer to a state hospital. Slowly, with the help of the public defender and the court psychiatrist, the facts of the case are revealed.

Merton, Vanessa. "Ethics Tests in the Legal Profession." <u>The Hastings Center Report</u>, 13:3 (June 1983), 27-31.

Contribution to a symposium on Ethics Tests for Medical Boards: The State of the Question. Merton discusses the Bar Admission Process; the Importance of "Character"; What Constitutes "Good Moral Character"; Ethics on the Bar Examination; the Multistate Professional Responsibility Examination; Objections to Standardized Ethics Tests; Opposition to Professional Testing; and An Unanticipated Problem. She concludes by suggesting that oral examinations in which candidates respond to videotaped clinical situations substitute for the usual perfunctory personal appearance before a character committee.

Meserve, Robert W., Francis C. Lynch and Lois B. Daniel. "The Devitt Report in Context: Public Responsibility of Lawyers in the 1980's." <u>University of Toledo Law Review</u> 11 (1980), 216-238.

Traces bar efforts from the 19th century to address problems of the competency of attorneys, delays and costs of legal services and public dissatisfaction with the administration of justice. The authors note that in 19th century England public dissatisfaction brought about legislative solutions to these problems. They warn that the bar's failure to deal with them in this country will lead to a similar result.

McGoff, Kevin P. "Disciplining Attorneys: Correcting No-

No's." _Res Gestae_ 25 (1981), 478-483.

Describes the procedure for disciplining attorneys under the Indiana Rules of Admission and Discipline. Rule 23 establishes a Disciplinary Commission through which the state Supreme Court exercises its jurisdiction in matters of attorney discipline.

Murphy, Francis T. Jr. "Grievance Counsel for the Public." _New York Law School Law Review_ 26 (1981), 221-236.

Proposes that the New York Supreme Court Appellate Division or the state legislature should establish a state wide lawyer discipline system. Such a system would separate prosecutorial and adjudicative functions and ensure uniform discipline throughout the state.

Note. "Access to the Disqualified Attorney's Work Product: A Plea For a Strict Prophylactic Rule." _University of Colorado Law Review_ 52 (1981), 465-487.

Discusses _First Wisconsin Mortgage Trust v. First Wisconsin Corporation_, a case in which counsel had been disqualified for joint representation. The client who was deprived of counsel by the disqualification sought access to the counsel's work product for the period of joint representation. The author argues that Canon 4 of the Code of Professional Responsibility requires that where the work product is tainted with confidentiality, the complaint should be dismissed based upon presumption that the work product will be misused.

Note. "Discipline of Attorneys in Maryland." _Maryland Law Review_ 35 (1975), 236-266.

Examines the source of the power to regulate attorneys: procedures for the bar association's surveillance and prosecution of attorney misconduct; and the standard of conduct judicially imposed through disciplinary proceedings.

Olmsted, Nancy K. "Law as a Business: The Impact of Title VII on the Legal Industry." _Valparaiso University Law Review_ 10 (1976), 478-506.

Starting from the premise that the practice of law is a business as well as a profession, Olmsted contends that the failure of legal employers to see themselves as businessmen leads to discrimination in legal employment.

She argues that Title VII, forbidding discrimination in hiring practices, also applies to legal employers.

Pfennigstorf, Werner and Spencer T. Kimball. "Regulation of Legal Service Plans." <u>American Bar Foundation Research Journal</u> 1977 (1977), 357-454.

Presents the results of a three-year study of alternative approaches to regulating legal services plans. The authors analyze the inherent dangers of various types of plans and suggest ways to provide protection for consumers. They recommend a system of insurance regulation, subject to appropriate amendments, to accommodate the unique features of some plans and special procedures to ensure close cooperation with disciplinary authorities on the conduct of lawyers.

Raven, Robert D. "President's Message." <u>California State Bar Journal</u> 56 (1981), 268-269.

The president of the state bar association publicizes the state's attorney discipline and complaint procedures, Client Security Fund and the alcohol-abuse program for attorneys. Raven describes legislation advocated by the bar relating to attorney discipline and competency.

Reichstein, Kenneth J. "Ambulance Chasing - a Case Study of Deviation and Control Within the Legal Profession." In <u>White Collar Criminal: The Defender in Business and the Professions</u>, ed. C. Geis. New York: Atherton Press, 1968.

Questions the validity of differentiating and separating the activities labeled crimes from those considered deviant conduct which may, in fact, have administrative consequences more severe than criminal sanctions. Reichstein analyzes attorney discipline cases decided by the Illinois Supreme Court which indicates that, in ambulance-chasing cases, the courts showed greater tolerance than displayed by the bar associations in their recommendations for attorney discipline.

Resh, Warren H. "Unfounded Attacks on Unauthorized Practice." <u>Unauthorized Practice News</u> 40 (1977), 272-279.

Addresses criticisms of the bar association's involvement in unauthorized practice enforcement. Resh argues that the courts have a strong interest in the enforcement of unauthorized practice prohibitions. He includes citations of numerous supporting cases.

Rhode, Deborah F. "Policing The Professional Monopoly: A Constitutional and Empirical Analysis of Unauthorized Practice Prohibitions." _Stanford Law Review_ 34 (1981), 1-112.

A history of unauthorized practice enforcement and an analysis of current enforcement activity, including the nature of bar enforcement and the participation of prosecutorial agencies. Rhode discusses the due process and First Amendment implications of unauthorized practice enforcement and criticizes the self-interested and circular standards that the legal profession has utilized over its history.

Rosenthal, Douglas. _A Model Peer Review System_. Philadelphia, PA: ALI-ABA Committee on Professional Competence and Responsibility, 1980.

Suggests procedures for evaluating attorney competence, the composition of a peer review group, proceedings for incompetence and disciplinary peer review.

Schwartz, Alan. "Automatic Discipline - A Concept Whose Time Has Arrived." _Detroit College of Law Review_ (Spring 1981), 1-28.

Describes the attorney discipline system in Michigan and a proposal to require automatic suspension of attorneys convicted of felonies. The history of automatic suspension in New York is outlined with emphasis on the treatment of felony convictions in other states and under federal law.

Schwartz, Daniel. "The New Legal Ethics and the Administrative Law Bar." From _The Good Lawyer_ ed. David Luban. Totowa, NJ: Rowman & Allanheld, 1984, pp. 236-256.

Focuses on important and difficult problems facing the administrative law bar, the group of lawyers who practice before administrative or regulating agencies and departments. Based upon his experience in practicing before government agencies, Schwartz delineates certain special features of administrative law, cites examples of the practical problems, discusses conflicts of interest, including the revolving door through which lawyers move between government and private practice. He concludes that some formal statement of legal ethics must be developed to limit abuses of the system, rather than leaving solutions to the conscience of lawyers.

Shuchman, Hedvah L. Self Regulation in the Professions: Accounting, Law, Medicine. Springfield, VA: National Technical Information Service, U.S. Dept. of Commerce, 1982.

Reports on research conducted from 1978 to 1981 comparing self-regulation to state regulation. Shuchman discusses three traditional prerequisites for entering a profession: education, experience and examinations. In law, school accreditation and the bar examination contribute to regulation, but the legal profession escapes review under "sunset" laws because it is mostly regulated by state supreme courts.

Slonim, Scott. "Are Lawyers Balking at True Self-Regulation?" American Bar Association Journal 66 (1980), 544-545.

Reaction to the proposed Model Rules of Professional Conduct has been negative, reports Slonin, since attorneys do not generally like to serve on disciplinary committees and since they perceive in the Rules a fundamental distrust of the attorney-client privilege. Lawyers have also reacted with disfavor to the Rules' mandatory pro bono provisions and the attendant requirement that pro bono work be reported.

Steele, Eric H. and Raymond T. Wimmer. "Lawyers, Clients, and Professional Regulation." American Bar Association Research Journal (1976), 917-1019.

Discusses public dissatisfaction with the profession, methods of maintaining professional discipline and the operation of disciplinary agencies in a number of states. The authors argue that a focus on deviance from professional norms and controls is unsatisfactory and they note a movement toward broader regulation involving administrative and dispute management methods.

Uviller, H. R. Processes of Criminal Justice -- Investigation and Adjudication. 2nd ed. Statutory Provisions and Proposals, and Ethical Problems. St. Paul, MN: West Publishing Co., 1979.

This supplement, intended for law students, presents proposed and enacted statutory provisions that address many of the questions raised or resolved in the judicial literature. Codifications of supplementary materials have been organized and keyed to the sequence of materials in the text. The concluding chapters present essays, standards and problems of ethical professional conduct by both prosecutor and defense counsel.

Walsh, Lawrence E. et al. "Price-Fixing, Advertising Bans, and Other Self-Regulation by Lawyers--What Future Under Anti-Trust Laws?" Columbia Journal of Law and Social Problems 12:4 (1976), 531-573.

Panel discussion of the impact of anti-trust laws on self-regulation by the organized bar in the wake of judicial decisions involving advertising bans and price-fixing by the bar associations. Several points of view are presented, including that of consumer groups. The authors criticize the bar's past handling of referral services.

Wolfram, Charles. "Barriers in Effective Public Participation in the Regulation of the Legal Profession." Minnesota Law Review 62 (1978), 619-647.

Argues the legal profession is uniquely insulated from the workings of the political process and that only the courts can exercise regulatory power. Nevertheless non-lawyers can influence regulation in three ways: 1) voluntary action by courts or bar associations; 2) congressional intervention; and 3) amendment of state constitutions to eliminate the negative aspect of the inherent powers doctrine. Reform, although no panacea, will at least renew public confidence. Wolfram notes that attempts by the public and the legislature to replace the present self-regulation of the bar will not necessarily succeed. A major preliminary step will be to discard the notion that the ethics of legal practice are so complex and intricate that only experts (lawyers) should attempt regulation. He also discusses the inherent powers doctrine whereby the courts have traditionally resisted attempts by other branches of government to regulate the practice of law.

D. LAWYERS AND SPECIAL GROUPS

Allison, Junius L. "Relationship Between the Office of Public Defender and the Assigned Counsel System." Valparaiso University Law Review 10 (1976), 399-422.

Describes three systems for affording indigents counsel in criminal adjudications: the public defender system, the assigned counsel system and a system which communicates with the public defender acting as an administrator assigning cases to staff attorneys and local counsel. Allison advocates the combined system and suggests standards by which judges may review its effectiveness.

American Bar Association. Counsel For Private Parties (Standards Relating to). Cambridge, MA: Ballinger, 1976.

Examines the juvenile justice system and its relationship to the rights and responsibilities of juveniles. The series is prepared under the supervision of a joint commission on juvenile justice standards appointed by the Institute of Judicial Administration and the ABA. A brief discussion of the past and current rules of counsel in the juvenile court is first presented. Standards are then listed on such aspects of juvenile representation as provision and organization of legal service, the lawyer-client relationship, the initial stages of representation and advising and counseling the client.

American Bar Foundation. Women Lawyers: Supplementary Data to the 1971 Statistical Report. Martha Grossblat and Bette H. Sikes, eds. Chicago: American Bar Foundation, 1973.

Statistical information concerning women lawyers profiling ages, job distributions, geographical distribution and other state and national statistical categories.

Andalman, Elliott and David L. Chambers. "Effective Counsel for Persons Facing Civil Commitment: A Survey, a Polemic and a Proposal." Mississippi Law Journal 45 (1974), 43-91.

Outlines systems for providing people facing civil commitment with effective counsel at a reasonable cost. It is based on a review of literature on systems in Chicago, Cleveland, New York and Memphis where counsel is regularly provided. The authors found attorneys provided by such services rarely expend much effort for their clients. In contrast they found attorneys working full time on commitment cases, where judges are sensitive to the freedoms that are imperiled, are often able to help their clients.

Boskey, James B. "Spousal Abuse in the United States." From Family Violence by John M. Eekelaar and Sanford N. Katz. Scarborough, Ontario, Canada: Butterworth, 1978.

In the United States, the role of the attorney in family violence is limited by the general reluctance of the courts to get involved in domestic disputes. This situation is contrasted with the reaction of the courts to child abuse. Here the interests of the state are defined more clearly and a full range of social and legal interventions are brought to bear on identified cases. Boskey urges attorneys in family practice to work for law reform to make divorce more easily obtainable, to work for shelters for abused spouses and their children, and to work for measures to require the abusing spouse to seek counseling.

Bourne, Richard. "Role of Attorneys on Child Abuse Teams." Chicago-Kent Law Review 54 (1978), 773-783.

Lawyers are reluctant to involve the courts in child abuse cases because of their conservative training, knowledge of the negative aspects of court action for both parents and child, and the difficulty in proving child abuse. The attorney's primary role in the hospital is to inform the staff of its legal obligations, yet the hospital staff is ambivalent about lawyers and the law. The hospital wants to avoid suit, yet feels that physicians, not lawyers, should make medical judgments. The lawyer must insure that abuse and neglect cases are processed according to all legal requirements. Another aspect of the lawyer's role on the trauma team is to prod governmental bureaucracies into action and to lobby for increased appropriations for children's services. The lawyers' role on the team is multidimensional and emotionally draining. But by respecting different professional views and showing the ability of the law to promote child protection, the abuse lawyer can contribute to the effective and humane case management of child abuse.

Brakel, Samuel J. "Free Legal Services for the Poor: Staffed Office vs. Judicare: The Client's Evaluation." Wisconsin Law Review 532 (1973).

Reports on a field study in the Judicare areas of Wisconsin and Montana and in the staffed-office area of the Upper Peninsula of Michigan. Compares clients' responses about their satisfaction with both the program and the handling of a case, and their nonprogram experiences.

Brakel, Samuel J. Judicare: Public Funds, Private Lawyers, and Poor People. Chicago, IL: American Bar Foundation, 1974.

The Judicare System, an experimental program for delivering legal services free of charge to poor people, is compared in northern Wisconsin and western Montana with the staffed-office program in the Upper Peninsula of Michigan. Brakel discusses the history of legal services, the problem of reaching the poor, the characteristics of lawyers in the program, the types of cases handled, the legal strategy employed by lawyers, the quality of service and the comparative costs.

Brakel, Samuel J. "Styles of Delivering Legal Services to the Poor: A Review Article." American Bar Foundation Research Journal 1 (1977), 219.

Critically examines Johnson's findings on alternative methods of delivering legal services to the poor as presented in Toward Equal Justice: A Comparative Study of Legal Aid in Modern Societies (edited by Mauro Cappelletti, James Gordley, and Earl Johnson, Jr.). Particular attention is given to methods of computing cost comparisons.

Brakel, Samuel J. "The Role of the Lawyer in the Mental Health Field." American Bar Foundation Research Journal 1977 (1977), 467-475.

Discusses the role of the lawyer in representing persons alleged to be mentally ill. Brakel believes a lawyer's duty in such cases is not adequately delineated by either the advocacy posture of counsel or a best-interest-of-the-client stance. In practice a lawyer must decide what legal services are most important to the client and then decide how to best use limited professional time, money and expertise.

Brakel, Samuel J. "Legal Aid in Mental Hospitals." American Bar Foundation Research Journal 1981 (1981), 23-93.

Analyzes a report based on the experiences of five in-hospital legal aid projects and one community based project for the deinstitutionalized. Brackel examines workloads of paralegals and lawyers in this setting and the approaches and predispositions they bring to the role or learn in it. He notes legal aid is useful and necessary but certain types of lawyering are counterproductive. The problems of clients in this setting are not appropriately handled by an overly adversarial approach. He explores the nature of these clients' problems and describes appropriate forms of legal services.

Brakel, Samuel, John Parry and Barbara Weiner, The Mentally Disabled and the Law. Chicago, IL: American Bar Association, 1961, 1971, 1984.

A standard reference work describing significant developments in policy, standards, practices and procedures for dealing with the mentally disabled. The revised edition in 1984 will include a sharper focus on the mentally retarded and a treatment of the new body of federal law in the area.

Bross, D. C. "Legal Advocacy for the Maltreated Child," Trial 14:7 (July 1978), 29-32, 68.

Discusses the attorney's role as counsel or guardian to an abused or otherwise maltreated child, and offers guidelines for effective child advocacy.

Burns, Hayward. "Racism and American Law." University of Toledo Law Review 2 (1970), 903-912.

Argues that legal education must be reevaluated so that law school training is more responsive to the demands of a changing society. Burns contends present teaching methods fail to put law into a social context. He describes a course, Racism and American Law, as an example of a positive curriculum change which deals with racism and its development in America as well as the potential of law for eliminating racism.

Carlin, Jerome and Jan Howard. "Legal Representation and Class Justice." University of California Los Angeles Law Review 12 (1965), 381-437.

Summarizes data on class differences in the use of lawyers and on the quality and integrity of the legal representation provided. The authors hypothesize that these differences result in a denial of justice to the poor since there are insufficient legal services available to assist them. They consider factors leading to inequality of legal representation and suggest conditions that must be met to provide adequate legal services to the poor. They conclude with a discussion of group legal service and neighborhood law offices.

Carter, Robert L. "The Black Lawyer." Humanist 29 (September-October 1969), 12-16.

Argues that though black lawyers played a central and major role in civil rights law cases in the 1950's, the subsequent opening of opportunities in private practice for talented black lawyers has removed them from that field. The civil rights attorney is now likely to be white and motivated by white values. Black lawyers need to regain their former pre-eminence in the field.

Cohen, Fred. "The Function of the Attorney and the Commitment of the Mentally Ill." Texas Law Review 44 (1966), 424-469.

Argues that although the legal profession is involved in commitment proceedings, the bar has abandoned any active participation in the system. As a consequence many are characterized as mentally ill and committed in a legal charade in which the lawyer merely goes through the motions. Cohen argues attorneys can play a central role in protecting clients' fundamental rights by vigorously participating in the proceedings.

Fendler, Oscar. "Utilization of Legal Manpower to Assist the Poor (Legal Aid)." Arkansas Law Review 25 (1971), 203-233.

Describes the history of legal aid, concentrating on the role of the Office of Economic Opportunity (OEO) and the controversy that has arisen between its defenders and members of the bar who advocate pro bono legal aid or pre-paid programs such as Wisconsin's Judicare. Fendler argues that a flexible federally funded system should be established that takes account of the fact that in many areas, an agency comparable to OEO may not be the best way to distribute legal services and reliance upon voluntary pro bono work by local attorneys should be encouraged.

Galie, Lawrence P. "An Essay On the Civil Commitment Lawyer: Or How I learned To Hate the Adversary System." Journal of Psychiatry and Law (Spring 1978), 71-87.

Discusses the dilemma facing an attorney charged with seeking the release of a respondent in a civil commitment proceeding who may need the treatment which commitment would bring. Galie examines the adversary role of the attorney and how it often conflicts with the best interests of the client. He argues that the problem of defending a client who is actually in need of medical care is more difficult for attorneys than defending a guilty client.

Hamilton, Guy, director, Man in the Middle. With Robert Mitchum and France Nuyen. Belmont, CA: Pennebaker, Inc., 1964.

Story of an American lieutenant who kills a British sergeant in India during World War II, aggravating partisan feelings between British and U.S. troops. The lieutenant's military attorney is ordered to rig the trial against the defendant in order to ease the tension. The attorney refuses and gets his client off for insanity.

Harrison, Michele Holovak. "Confidentiality of Attorney-Client Consultations in the Prison Setting." New England Journal of Prison Law 3:2 (Spring 1977), 539-548.

The prisoner's right of access to the courts is the basis for guaranteed confidential oral communications between prisoners and lawyers. The right to private consultation is not absolute and is limited by the need to maintain prison security and discipline. Three major factors have limited the right to private consultation: the presence of third-party observers at prisoner-lawyer consultations; the use of listening devices by the authorities; and the physical facilities available for use in consulations. To protect the prisoner's right to private consultation with his attorney, the courts have allowed only visual observation of the interview by prison personnel. Use of eavesdropping devices has been held in direct conflict with confidentiality requirements.

Herman, Robert , Eric Single and John Boston. *Counsel for the Poor: Criminal Defense in Urban America*. Lexington, MA: Lexington Books, 1977.

Reports on a study of criminal defense lawyers in New York, Washington, DC and Los Angeles who represent indigents. The authors attempt to evaluate the effectiveness of lawyers from legal aid in public defender organizations, court appointed counsel, and lawyers who represent paying clients.

James, Marlise. *The People's Lawyers*. New York: Holt, Rinehart and Winston, 1973.

Describes the activities of lawyers, organizations, firms, and collectives who represent the disadvantaged or are active in civil rights and civil liberties advocacy. James also discusses lawyers' associations with such groups as the NAACP, the Black Panther Party, United Farm Workers and the Native American Rights Fund.

Johnson, Earl. "Professional Responsibility Aspects of Legal Services Programs." *University of Colorado Law Review* 41 (1969), 319-327.

Discusses the role played by the Office of Economic Opportunity legal services projects in encouraging lawyers and law students to exercise and be educated in their professional responsibilities. Legal services programs have participated in numerous test cases which have challenged laws thought to be unfair to the poor. Examines the Legal Aid Society in New York City.

Mulligan, Robert, director. *To Kill A Mockingbird*. With Gregory Peck, Mary Badham, and Phillip Alford. Pakula-Mulligan Productions - Brentwood Productions, 1962. 129 min.

In a small Alabama town in 1932, Atticus Finch, a widowed lawyer, strives to create for his two children an atmosphere free from hatred and prejudice. Finch agrees to defend Tom Robinson, a Negro accused of raping a young white girl. Although he is able to demonstrate Robinson's innocence, the all-white jury returns a verdict of guilty.

National Council of Juvenile and Family Court Judges. "Role of Lawyer in Juvenile Court." By D.W. Bahlmann and R.A. Ortique. Chicago, IL: Teach 'Em Inc., 1976. (audio cassette)

This tape cassette from the Third National Conference on Juvenile Justice presents three possible models for the role of the lawyer in the juvenile court: (1) deeming the attorney to be an assistant of the court, taking only positions which advocate the best interest of the child; (2) having the attorney assume an advocate role similar to that of a defense counsel in a criminal case; and (3) acting as an advisor to the client, or providing an alternative person as advisor.

Note. "The Role of Counsel in the Civil Commitment Process: A Theoretical Framework." Yale Law Journal 84 (1975), 1540-1563.

Notes that most states now provide counsel for individuals subject to commitment proceedings. The author argues that the counsel's role is undefined, a problem that stems from the essentially paternalistic approach of all parties involved in such proceedings. In helping an attorney to choose between the roles of advocate and mere representative, the author discusses the requirements of the Code of Professional Responsibility and case law regarding the motive of effective counsel. He believes that the lawyer should vigorously challenge the opinions of committing psychiatrists.

Reinhardt, Gottfried. Town Without Pity. With Kirk Douglas and E. G. Marshall. Mirisch Corp. 1961. 105 min.

A 16 year old girl is brutally raped by four drunken GI's from the U.S. occupation forces. Outraged, the girl's father demands that the military impose the death penalty, a verdict possible only if the girl testifies. The defense counsel warns the father that he will do all in his legal power to save the men's lives, even if it means subjecting his daughter to vicious cross examination and destroying her reputation. At the trial, the defense attorney uses the testimonies of vindictive witnesses to establish the girl as a tease. While on the stand he ruthlessly badgers and taunts the girl until she collapses. Unable to finish her testimony, the soldiers receive long prison sentences. The defense attorney later learns that the young girl has committed suicide.

The Bill of Rights in Action: Juvenile Law. CBS; BFA. 1974 (film). 24 min.

Explores the juvenile detention system in relation to the adult offender's ability to be released on bail and also the constitutionality of the laws concerning juvenile detention and prosecution. Presents two adolescents being arrested in connection with the robbery of an elderly lady at knife point. Shows a juvenile court hearing and the arguments presented at the court hearing requesting a writ of habeas corpus for the juvenile offender.

Schwartz, Helene E. Lawyering. New York: Farrar, Straus & Giroux, 1975.

A woman lawyer discusses the work involved in political and constitutional litigation. She describes her involvement in numerous cases representing clients from all parts of the political spectrum. She explains the preparation that goes into litigating a constitutional case and brings to each chapter her observations on how her sex may have been a liability in doing her job.

Smith, Reginald H. Justice and The Poor. New York: Scribner's, 1919.

One of the first important studies attacking the denial of justice to the poor.

Sparer, Edward V. "The Role of the Welfare Client's Lawyer." University of California Los Angeles Law Review 12 (1965), 361-380.

Outlines problems that beset welfare recipients in securing and maintaining their entitlements. Sparer discusses the function of an attorney representing the poor and the difficulties that the client's poverty and powerlessness raise. He notes that attorneys become embroiled in ethical problems in this sort of practice because the ethical tenets governing legal practice tend to discourage active assistance to indigent clients.

White, James J. "Women in the Law." Michigan Law Review 65 (1967), 1051-1122.

Examines the status of women in the legal profession, what they do compared with men, and the forces that might narrow the gap between male and female status. White discusses problems encountered by women in the practice of law including a lack of client confidence in a female attorney.

CHAPTER FIVE
THE COURTS

A. JUDICIAL CONDUCT

Alexander, Harry T. "Court Monitoring - A Necessity." From *Crime and Its Impact on the Black Community* by Lawrence E. Gary and Lee P. Brown. Washington: Howard University Institute for Urban Affairs and Research, 1976. 11 p.

A court monitoring system is discussed as a means for curbing abuses of the criminal justice system by judges, prosecutors, and defense attorneys.

American Bar Association. *Code of Judicial Conduct*. Chicago, IL: American Bar Association, 1972. 32p.

The code consists of statements of norms denominated canons, accompanying text setting forth specific rules, and commentary.

Ashman, C. R. *Finest Judges Money Can Buy*. Los Angeles, CA: Nash Publishing Corp., 1973.

Documents numerous instances of judicial corruption and misconduct. Ashman points out cases in which judges are linked to mafia pay-offs, nepotism, sexual license and other favors, and abuse of authority.

Belliotti, Raymond A. "Values in the Courtroom." *Westminster Institute Review* 1:3 (October 1981), 3-5.

Faults the adversarial system for the moral schitzophrenia lawyers suffer, society's cynical view of the legal profession and process, and the vast disparity between the factually and declared guilty. Defends instead an inquisitorial system in which the guilty accused has a moral responsibility to acknowledge his deeds and which places a higher premium on the discovery of the truth. Belliotti believes a more inquisitorial system would discourage witness manipulation plea bargaining and encourage more trust between society and the accused.

Bollens, John C. and Henry J. Schmandt, "Even the Judiciary," in *Political Corruption: Power, Money and Sex*.

Pacific Palisades, CA: Palisades Publishers, 1979, pp. 163-179.

Braithwaite, William T. Who Judges the Judges? Chicago, IL: American Bar Foundation, 1971.

Braithwaite gives an overview of the problems of judicial misconduct and disability and then focuses on the way California, Illinois, Missouri, New Jersey and New York handle instances of alleged judicial unfitness, ranging from public charges of criminal misconduct through the more common allegations of physical disability resulting from advanced age. Braithwaite notes the advantages and disadvantages of each state's answer to the question.

Coen, George W. "A Look at Lawyer Discipline in Ohio." Capital University Law Review 7 (No. 2, 1977), 245-253.

A member of the Ohio Supreme Court's Board of Commissioners on Grievances and Discipline discusses the "inordinate publicity" of misconduct which, he contends, threatens the entire legal profession's reputation. He defends the bar's disciplinary procedures, but believes the Ohio disciplinary plan does not adequately protect the "good name of the profession." He recommends that the bar adopt three preventive measures: (1) the establishment of a trust account to reduce commingling of funds; (2) submission of proof of the filing of income tax returns as a prerequisite to registration; and (3) a means for allowing a mentally ill lawyer to temporarily relinquish his license while undergoing treatment. The authors select three cases to illustrate judicial misconduct. The first involves judge Mitchell Schweitzer in the underworld influence on the courts. In the second judges Roy Solfisburg and Ray Klingbiel are involved in bribery at the appellate level. In the third judge Maxwell Willens was indicted and convicted of corruption. While acknowledging the general integrity of judges, the authors urge that miscreant judges be treated the same as any public official accused of wrongdoing.

Davis, Evan A. and Alisa F. Levin. "Disqualifying Judges." Litigation 7:52 (Winter 1981), 11-14.

Discusses grounds for judicial disqualification and offers to guide an attorney on how and when to seek disqualification.

Downie, Leonard, Jr. Justice Denied -- The Case for Reform of the Courts. Penguin Books, 1979.

Criticism of practices, inefficiencies, and inequities of the American Trial Court System, based on visits to courts across the nation, interviews with court officials and attorneys, and intensive research into court reform literature. Downie discusses current proposals for court reform.

Dworkin, Ronald M. "Judicial Discretion." Journal of Philosophy 60 (Oct. 1963), 624-638.

To the layperson, judges should and in general do, "find the law and not make it." The academic branch of the legal profesion seems agreed that the layperson is mistaken, that judges must sometimes reach their decisions by means other than the application of standards, that such standards leave them free to "choose." The purpose of this paper is to argue that this professional opinion is an inaccurate way to describe the facts and that the layperson's opinion, while deceptively suggesting that adjudication is simple, is closer to the truth.

Dworkin, Ronald. "Wasserstrom: The Judicial Decision." Ethics 75 (Oct. 1964), 47-56.

In The Judicial Decision Richard Wasserstrom searches for an ideal decision procedure. This search produces a two-level procedure which involves first deciding which relevant rule of law best promotes the function of the legal system and second applying that rule to the case. The assumption that the law must serve some overriding function, such as utility, is dubious and is not recognized in jurisprudential practice. It rests upon the further, questionable assumption that to the extent that courts make law, the same standards of lawmaking apply to them as to legislatures.

Gallas, Geoffrey and Michael Lampasi. "A Code of Ethics for judicial Administrators." Judicature 61 (Feb. 1978), 311-317.

The authors contend that court administrators cannot rely on other professions' standards. They cite examples of situations in which court administrators did not meet the ethical challenges of their positions. Ethics should be analyzed by focusing on four aspects: principles; codes; matters of professional propriety and appropriateness; and professional/advisory opinions. Eight canons for court administrators are proposed which address the following matters: preserving independence of the courts, promoting integrity and impartiality of the courts, avoiding conflict of interest, performing duties efficiently and effectively, advocating for improved court management, abstaining from partisan political activities that impair professional performance, safeguarding security and privacy of court records, and maintaining primary allegiance to the public, rather than to the organization.

Greenberg, Frank. "Task of Judging the Judges." Judicature 59:10 (May 1976), 458-467.

Examines the reasons behind the development of judicial disciplinary systems, the ends to which the systems are properly dedicated, and the ways in which they can best discharge their responsibilities.

Hinsdale, C. E. "Summary of the Judicial Standards Commission's Work." Popular Government 44:3 (Winter 1979), 42-44.

In this 1977 report, the Judicial Standards Commission of North Carolina summarizes the activities for its first five years. The Commission handled 215 complaints against judges, reprimanded seven judges, and censured five.

Jackson, Donald Dale. Judges. New York: Atheneum, 1974.

Portrays judges as people whose personalities, background, political and social affiliations, values, experiences, and legal competence affect the way each exercises judicial power. The failures most prevalent in judges are seen to be intellectual inadequacy, corruption, bigotry, tyranny, temperamental instability, and physical or mental disabilities.

Kramer, Stanley, dir. Judgment at Nuremburg. With Spencer Tracy and Burt Lancaster. Roxlom Films, 1961.

An American judge presides at the trial of several German judges who supported Hitler's racist policies. The defense maintains that the judges were guilty only of upholding the law, and cannot be held culpable unless the entire nation is considered guilty. U.S. military officals hint that leniency for the Germans would encourage western solidarity in face of growing East-West tension.

Lauter, David. "A Judge for a Client." National Law Journal (Feb. 7, 1983), 1, 10-11, 21.

On December 29th, 1981, a black federal U.S. District Court judge, Alcee Hastings, was indicted on conspiracy to bribe and obstruction of justice charges. The charges centered around the trial of two brothers who had been convicted in Judge Hastings' court the previous December of bilking New Jersey teamsters' pension fund of $1 million. Hastings had ordered the brothers to forfeit their $323,000 interest in a restaurant and $845,000 in cash proceeds from their racketeering scheme. According to Hastings, defense attorney William Borders, a friend, invited him to dinner on September 16th, 1981 and stood him up. A team of FBI agents, however, although uninvited, were present. Borders, four days earlier, had met with an FBI agent whom he mistakenly believed to be Frank Romano, one of the brothers. Borders, on Hastings behalf, had allegedly contacted the brothers to solicit a bribe in return for a reduced sentence and the return of the $845,000. On September 20th Hastings signed an order returning $845,000 to the brothers. But, unbeknown to the brothers, a key ruling rendered on June 19th, 1981, established new law which did not allow the forfeiture of simple cash proceeds. This ruling is the center of Hastings' defense. Under it he had no choice but to return the $845,000. The author asks "was Alcee Hastings set up and betrayed by an unscrupulous friend and persecuted by a white establishment . . . or is he the latest in a long, sad list of federal officials . . . who have cashed in on public prominence for private gain?" Hastings is representing himself with the help of an inexperienced black female attorney.

Levy, Harold S. "Judicial Recusals." Pace Law Review 2 (Winter 1982), 35-46.

Vice President of New York Telephone and Telegraph discusses the inability of judges to hear cases involving corporate clients based either on extraordinarily strict ethical standards or on broad interpretations of 'non-mandatory' disqualification circumstances. He covers both mandatory disqualification situations involving financial interest, and non-mandatory situations like prior representation of a client or prior membership in a law firm. Stock ownership in A.T. & T. is cited as a prime example of financial interest. Such interest, Levy contends, can result in the same few judges hearing all of a corporation's cases and serve as an excuse to avoid hearing difficult cases. He suggests that a judge should be allowed to hear the case if the parties to litigation wave recusal.

Mackenzie, John P. Appearance of Justice. NY: Charles Scribner's Sons, 1974.

Discusses incidents where the ethical behavior of federal judges has been questioned and recommends improvements in defining and enforcing ethical behavior. Mackenzie maintains that even the outward appearance of the behavior of judges in private as well as professional life should measure up to certain moral criteria.

Mackenzie, John P. "Of Judges and the ABA." From Verdicts on Lawyers by Ralph Nader and Mark Green. New York: Thomas Y. Crowell, 1976, 33-46.

The weaknesses and strengths of the American Bar Association role in the judicial selection process are examined and the role of the legal profession in selection is discussed.

Meacham, Ruth A. "The Legal Profession - Appeals Promised Upon Ethical Grounds." University of Toledo Law Review 11 (1980), 473-510.

Discusses judicial treatment of ethical standards when a client appeals on grounds that an attorney's unethical conduct has prejudiced his substantive rights. The court's decision must be based on the rights of the injured party. But the clients have used ethical standards to measure permissible conduct in appeals based on malpractice or failure to disqualify, and in cases involving the conduct of public attorneys.

Pound, Roscoe. "Justice According to Law." Columbia Law Review 13 (1913), 696-713.

Contains Dean Pound's thoughts on the necessity of balancing the rule of law with the exercise of discretion by judges in order to resolve disputes justly. He views the two to be in unending dialectic with the rule of law regularly asserted to curb excessive judicial liberalization and discretion, mitigating the harsh results of law that has grown too rigid.

Ranhi, David. "How Should Judges Be Disciplined?" National Law Journal 5 (No.21, Jan. 30 1983), 1, 26-28.

Staff reporter says "disciplinary proceedings against state judges are coming out of the closet." According to Judicial Conduct Organizations 19 states now require public hearings after formal charges have been filed, up from nine only five years ago. Ranhi discusses various responses to the commissions, the press's role, arguments for and against open proceedings and confidentiality.

Rindolph, F. Lyman. The Country Lawyer: Essays in Democracy. Philadelphia: University of Pennsylvania Press, 1938.

Describes the pleasures and satisfactions of a general practice in law in a small community. Rindolph contrasts the character of such a practice with that of lawyers in a metropolitan setting, arguing that the country lawyer's intimate contacts with all sorts and conditions of men in the vicissitudes of life afford him a deeper knowledge of human nature.

Rosett, Arthur. "The Changing Judiciary." Kentucky Law Journal 69 (Fall 1980-81), 843-868.

A professor of law at the University of California, Los Angeles, argues "the judiciary is being transformed into a group of professional technicians and civil servants operating within large centralized bureaucracies, cut off from supporting local, political and professional ties." He believes this increased trend toward centralization and bureaucracy threatens judicial autonomy. He suggests "assessment of the judge by the community in which the court operates could be an important tool to redress the balance of political influence on the judge and to maintain the political accountability of the individual judge."

Sneed, Joseph T. "When Should the Lions Be on the Throne? Reflections on Judicial Supremacy." Arizona Law Review 21 (1979), 925-944.

Ninth circuit court judge charges that Supreme Court judges shape the Constitution and use it to regulate too many activities. He offers four suggestions to strengthen the legitimacy of judicial review by improving constitutional coherence. First, avoid popular judicial control because it threatens coherence. Second, use the Framers' Original Intent as an interpretive baseline. Third, depart from the original intent only for those without access to the political process. Fourth, avoid constitutional change when it would require the courts to assume wide ranging supervisory responsibilities. Sneed concludes that "the effective power of the judiciary depends upon its doing the job properly."

Stern, Robert L. "Comment [on Judicial Ethics]." University of Chicago Law School Conference Series, Proceedings of the Conference on Judicial Ethics, 22 Oct. 1964 (No. 19, 1965), 17-24.

An attorney comments on Judge Hastings' "Judicial Ethics as it Relates to Participation in Money-making Activities." Canon 26 says that a judge should not invest "in enterprises which are apt to be involved in litigation." Although broad interpretations could preclude all investments, Stern contends that judges have not interpreted it that way. Canon 29 states "a judge should not sit where his personal interests are involved." After presenting several situations, Stern concludes that the judge's conscience, not rules, must guide his actions.

Tribe, Laurence H. "Courts Should Not Be Criticized for Ignoring Public Opinion." California Lawyer 2 (Jan. 1982), 11-12.

A professor of Law at Harvard argues that judges must adhere to the law, not public opinion. Tribe takes issue with Preble Stolz's Judging Judges, which he contends fails to address the most significant issues in the California experiences in People vs. Tanner. "One must stand aghast at the basic philosophy that (U.S. Attorney General William French) Smith and Stolz seem to share: the courts, to which we entrust the solemn task of interpreting and enforcing constitutional provisions, however imprecisely expressed, owe their allegiance not to the law as they understand it, but to the shifting sands of public opinion.

Volcansek, Mary T. "Codes of Judicial Ethics: Do They Affect Judges' Views of Proper Off-the-Bench Behavior?" American Business Law Journal 17 (1980), 493-505.

Analyses responses to questionnaire sent to Texas judges to examine their perceptions of the propriety of judicial action in business and political milieus in light of recent revisions to judicial code.

Wallace, J. Clifford. "The Jurisprudence of Judicial Restraint: a Return to the Moorings." George Washington Law Review 50 (Nov. 1981), 1-16.

A U.S. Court of Appeals judge for the 9th Circuit argues that judicial restraint preserves constitutional precepts, supports the separation of powers, protects democracy and preserves fundamental rights. Wallace admits that adherence to this philosophy would not allow judges to right every wrong. Law making, he suggests, should be left to legislators.

Wiley, Jerry. "The Impact of Judicial Decisions On Professional Conduct: An Empirical Study." Southern California Law Review 55 (1982), 345-396.

Attempts to evaluate the impact of judicial decisions on the behavior of a group affected by a decision. Wiley discusses a Washington court's pronouncement that opthomologists should routinely test patients for glaucoma as the basis for a study of compliance by the affected professionals.

Wyzanski, Charles E. Whereas - A Judge's Premises: Essays in Judgment, Ethics, and the Law. Boston: Little, Brown, 1965.

This collection of addresses and essays by a judge includes the responsibility of the trial judge; appraisals of the careers of learned and Augustus Hand and Louis Brandeis; Constitutionalism and the role of lawyers in an age of social legislation.

B. PROSECUTORIAL DISCRETION

Aron, C. "Prosecutorial Misconduct - A National Survey." *De Paul Law Review* 21 (1971), 422-484.

Analyses the case law evolving from the 1935 Supreme Court decision in *Mooney v. Hologan*, which held that the prosecutor's knowing use of perjured testimony violated the defendant's due process rights. Aron discusses the scope of the rights and responsibilities of both prosecution and defense as defined through subsequent case law.

Chesler, L. M. "Relationship of the Prosecutor with the Private Defense Counsel." From *Prosecutorial Relationships in Criminal Justice* by John Jay Douglass. Houston, TX: National College of District Attorneys, College of Law, University of Houston, 1977, 65-92.

The relationships of the prosecutor with the private defense counsel are examined, taking into consideration the need for respect within an adversarial relationship, the need for cooperation, negotiations, and the prosecutor's ethical responsiblities.

Douglass, John J., ed. *Ethical Considerations in Prosecution -- Roles and Functions of the Prosecutor*. Houston, TX: National College of District Attorneys, 1977.

Codes, court decisions, professional canons, and statutes relating to the moral responsibilities of the prosecutor are reprinted with focus on documents establishing the philosophical basis of prosecutorial conduct. A bibliography with over 60 citations and some footnotes are included.

Goldstein, Abraham S. *The Passive Judiciary: Prosecutorial Discretion and the Guilty Plea*. Baton Rouge, LA: Louisiana State University Press, 1981.

Argues that judges should take a more active role in court proceedings, and prosecutors a less active one, and offers recommendations on how to accomplish this.

Justice Under the Law. TCF. 1947. 35 min.(film).

An abridged version of the film *Boomerang*. Emphasizes the duty of a prosecuting attorney to protect the innocents as well as to punish the guilty. When a man is charged with murder on the basis of circumstantial evidence alone, the prosecutor resists political pressure and disproves the evidence. Shows various legal steps in a murder case.

Uviller, H. Richard. "Virtuous Prosecutor in Quest of an Ethical Standard: Guidance From the ABA." Michigan Law Review 71:6 (May 1973), 1145-1168.

Examines the ethical problems in selective prosecution, prejudgment of credibility and conflict of interest. Uviller argues that a prosecutor should disqualify himself from cases in which his loyalty may be perceived as divided between his duty and personal advantage. He concludes that while a prosecutor should not regularly prosecute cases where he is not convinced that the evidence points to guilt, nor should he, in the face of personal uncertainty, refrain from submitting evidence to the dialectic of the judicial process.

C. PLEA BARGAINING

Alschuler, Albert W. "Courtroom Misconduct by Prosecutors and Trial Judges." Texas Law Review 50:4(April 1972), 629-735.

Reviews the traditional remedies for serious misconduct by prosecutors and trial judges. Alschuler suggests that the best corrective for prosecutorial misconduct may be punishment for contempt of court. Statutory grounds for disqualification of trial judges might be enacted or provision might be made for the abolition of absolute judicial immunity, thus subjecting trial judges to civil lawsuits.

Alschuler, Albert W. "Defense Attorney's Role in Plea Bargaining." Yale Law Journal 84:6 (May 1975), 1179-1313.

Explores the extent to which the presence of counsel provides a significant safeguard of fairness in guilty plea negotiation, and finds that current conceptions of the defense attorney's role are more romanticized than real. Alschuler believes plea bargaining is an inherently irrational method of administering justice and destructive of sound attorney-client relationships. He contends that this system subjects defense attorneys to serious temptations to disregard their clients' interests. The author concludes that nothing short of abolition of plea bargaining promises satisfactory resolution of these problems.

Alschuler, Albert W. "Plea Bargaining and its History." Columbia Law Review 79:1 (Jan. 1979), 1-43.

Although documentation is incomplete, analysis of past court cases indicates that judicial discouragement of confessions, lack of counsel for defendants, and prescribed penalties for felonies all militated against plea bargaining until after the U.S. Civil War. Surveys in the 1920"s indicated guilty plea percentages in convictions ranged from 74 percent to 90 percent in major U.S. cities. In later years, the growing percentage of reduction of charges in return for guilty pleas indicates that prosecutors may have offered greater concessions in return for guilty pleas. Alschuler concludes the growth in plea bargaining is the result of higher costs; urbanization, increasing crime rates, expansion of substantive criminal law, and professionalization and bureaucratization of police and prosecutors.

Alschuler, Albert W. "The Prosecutor's Role in Plea Bargaining." University of Chicago Law Review 36 (1968), 50-112.

Examines the factors prosecutors weigh in offering to plea bargain: trial strategy, interactions with defense counsel, political and quasi-judicial motivations, the strength of their case and the type of crime. Alschuler contends the informality of the system encourages improper motives by the plea bargaining parties.

Alschuler, Albert W. "The Supreme Court, the Defense Attorney, and the Guilty Plea." University of Colorado Law Review 47 (1975), 1-71.

Discusses the Supreme Court's rejection of challenges to guilty-plea convictions in three cases: McMann v. Richardson, Parker v. North Carolina, and Brady v. United States. In all three cases defendants were represented by counsel, a factor on which the court based its implicit conclusion that a competently counseled guilty plea could be presumed knowing and voluntary. The critical issue was the effectiveness of legal representation for defendants. Alschuler is highly critical of the results.

Alschuler, Albert W. "Trial Judge's Role in Plea Bargaining, Part I." Columbia Law Review 76:7 (Nov. 1976), 1059-1154.

Commentaries on judicial participation in plea bargaining cover systems in which prosecutors completely dominate plea bargaining and judges do not participate; and systems in which there is no explicit bargaining but to those defendants who do not take their cases to trial; system in which judges participate but avoid specific promises. Include more judicial control of sentencing promises, negotiation in the defendant's presence and negotiation based on the sentence to be imposed rather than on the number and level of charges.

Beall, George. "Principles of Plea Bargaining." Loyola University Law Review 9:1 (Fall 1977), 175-192.

The most common bargaining practice is "charge bargaining," where the defendant tenders a plea of guilty of nolo contendre to one charge in return for a prosecutorial commitment to drop, reduce, or refrain from bringing additional charges. "Sentence bargaining" occurs when the defendant pleads guilty to the original charge in return for a recommendation from the prosecutor of sentencing concessions. Various bargaining points of the prosecutor include reduction of the original charge, dismissal of other charges, recommendation of probation or other leniency, agreement to make no recommendations regarding sentence or not to oppose a defense plea of leniency, agreement to dismiss charges against a codefendant, and stipulation to a specific sentence, such as restitution or incarceration in a penal institution. Beall believes the adversary system makes pressure to bargain irresistible. Judicial participation in plea bargaining is significant, even though negotiations are invariably conducted between defense counsel and prosecutor. No formal ethical guidelines exist for defense counsel and prosecutors regarding the substance of plea bargaining, but Beall believes an advocate must deal honestly and without exaggeration.

Brunk, Conrad G. "The Problem of Voluntariness and Coercion in the Negotiated Plea." Law and Society 13 (1979), 527-553.

Argues that in many cases negotiations to reduce sentences are just as coercive as those involving threats of punishment. Though a negotiated plea is not necessarily involuntary, both aspects must be considered and eliminated before finding it voluntary.

"Conditional Guilty Pleas." Harvard Law Review 93:3 (Jan. 1980), 564-585.

Presents the argument that conditional guilty pleas are permissible, that they represent sound judicial policy, and that the Constitution compels courts to give criminal defendants this plea-bargaining option.

Heumann, Milton. Plea Bargaining: The Experiences of Prosecutors, Judges, and Defense Attorneys. Chicago, IL: University of Chicago Press, 1978.

A study of the process by which newly recruited defense attorneys, prosecutors, and judges adapt to the use of plea bargaining. The experiences of both defense attorneys and prosecutors are traced from their recruitment through the final stages of their adaptation to the plea bargaining process. Describes their intitial expectations regarding court trials, the adversary relationship, and, for defense attorneys, the innocense of most of their future clients. Examines their evolving perceptions of guilt and the development of their ability to distinguish among guilty defendants, along with the ways in which new attorneys first learn how to go about plea bargaining and how their opinions of its purpose, usefulness, and morality change at different stages of experience. Judges are also conditioned to accept plea bargaining, and the process by which their adaptation occurs is analyzed as well. Suggestions for a plea bargaining reform policy are presented, and recommendations are made for further research. The book contains notes, a bibliography,and an index.

Joo Shin, J. "Do Lesser Pleas Pay?: Accommodations in the Sentencing and Parole Processes." Journal of Criminal Justice 1 (1973), 27-42.

Analyzes differences in sentence lengths or in actual periods of incarceration according to such variables as original charge, type of plea, conviction charge, and magnitude of charge reductions. Study indicates that charge reduction may reduce the actual amount of time served, but the parole process tends to neutralize the sentence differentials.

Katsh, E., R. M. Pipkin, and B. S. Katsh. Plea Bargaining -- A Game of Criminal Justice. Springfield, MA: Legal Studies Simulations, 1980. (multi-media game kit)

Designed for use at the college level, this game is a role playing simulation of the plea bargaining process. It encourages law students to actively study the reasons for plea bargaining, examine alternatives to it, and learn how the system works. Participants act out the roles of district attorney, judge, public defender, and accused. The sentences resulting from the plea bargaining process are eventually revealed, along with the actual innocence or guilt of the accused, and a debriefing discussion is held after the game is over.

Kipnis, Kenneth. "Criminal Justice and the Negotiated Plea." Ethics 86 (Jan. 1976), 93-106.

Plea bargains, which have become the standard way of disposing of criminal cases, have no proper place in the American Criminal Justice system. Relying on the doctrine of duress, it is argued that plea agreements may be involuntary by virtue of prosecutorial inducements now incorrectly considered proper by the Supreme Court. It is shown that, except in serendipitous circumstances, justice, the administration of deserved punishment, will never be the outcome of the plea bargaining procedure. Kipnis argues that under plea bargaining there is inadequate reason to believe that the convicted are guilty.

McDonald, William F. and James A. Cramer, eds. Plea-Bargaining. Lexington, MA: Lexington Books, 1980.

Presents major findings of original, unpublished research on plea bargaining, including reports on experiments in Texas, Alaska, Florida, and England. Also discussed is a three year national study conducted by the Institute of Criminal Law and Procedure at Georgetown University which focused on plea bargaining in the state courts. A review of sentence-bargaining in federal district courts is presented, and a project in the district of Columbia which examined plea bargaining by using the detailed data base in the prosecutor management information system is reported. Finally, plea bargaining in England is examined. Tables, reference notes, an index, and a list of contributors are provided.

Newman, Donald J. and Edgar C. NeMoyer. "Issues of Propriety in Negotiated Justice." Denver Law Journal 47:3 (1970), 367-405.

Discusses present and potential abuses of plea-bargaining. The authors believe that if the states act affirmatively to base charge and sentence concessions on proper motivations then plea bargaining can survive.

Parker, James F. "Plea Bargaining." American Journal of Criminal Law (1972), 187-209.

Describes extant plea bargaining practices and criticizes the rationale for plea bargaining, the coercive tactics of prosecutors, the presumption that defendants have knowingly waived constitutional trial rights, and its overall effects upon the criminal justice system.

Wertheimer, Alan. "Freedom, Morality, Plea Bargaining, and the Supreme Court." Philosophy and Public Affairs 8 (Spring 1979), 203-234.

The Supreme Court has ruled that guilty pleas induced by plea bargaining are voluntary. Wertheimer argues that the Court has developed a sound conceptual account of voluntariness, namely, to say that a defendant voluntarily pleads guilty requires moral judgments about the "state"'s behavior. Wertheimer believes the Court has misapplied that theory and has made several incorrect moral judgments about plea bargaining.

Wertheimer, Alan. "The Prosecutor and the Gunman." Ethics 89 (April 1979), 269-279.

Kenneth Kipnis argued that a defendant's decision to accept a plea-bargain is analogous to accepting a gunman's proposal to spare one's life in exchange for one's money: such a decision is made under duress and is not compatible with the right to a trial by jury. Author shows that this argument cannot be sustained: if a prosecutor's offer constitutes duress, it does not do so in the way a gunman's proposal constitutes duress.

Wishingrad, Jay. "The Plea Bargain in Historical Perspective." Buffalo Law Review 23 (1974), 499-507.

Traces the evolution of the custom of plea bargaining

and related informal aspects of the criminal process from earliest times to the present. Wishingrad examines several cases expressing American attitudes toward this practice. He discusses the attitudes of judges, prosecutors and defendant's attorneys.

D. DISCLOSURE

American Bar Association. Consortium For Professional Education. "Investigation." Videotape (60 min.), Vignette (10 min.).

Dramatizes a collection suit involving the refusal to continue payments on the purchase of a defective used car. The defendant's attorney visits one of the plaintiff's witnesses and learns much that he can and does use against the witness in court. Several issues are raised including attorney preparation, discovery, the right to interview opposing witnesses, fairness, and breach of trust.

Fedders, John M., and Lauryn H. Guttenplan. "Document Retention and Destruction - Practical, Legal and Ethical Considerations." <u>Notre Dame Lawyer</u> 56:1 (1980), 5-64.

Discusses the risk of criminal liability when corporations regularly dispose of business records, thereby frustrating anti-trust law enforcement. Applicable federal, state, municipal and foreign law is discussed. The authors consider Congressional proposals to regulate these practices and an attorney's ethical considerations in counseling destruction of documents where some risk of adverse evidentiary inference exists.

"Legal Ethics and the Destruction of Evidence." <u>Yale Law Journal</u> 88:8 (July 1979), 1665-1688.

Argues that the code of professional responsibility should be amended to cover evidence destruction. Attorneys should not be free to change the nature of the facts available to future adversaries, which is the effect of destroying evidence. Such actions threaten basic assumptions about the adversary system. The attorney-client privilege should not protect the contents of documents when the attorney advised or assisted in their destruction. It is suggested that some enforcement mechanism is needed to ensure compliance with the rule.

Note. "Disclosure of Incriminating Physical Evidence Received From a Client: The Defense Attorney's Dilemma: University of Colorado Law Review 52 (1981), 419-463.
Discusses the legal and ethical obligations of an attorney to disclose incriminating evidence received from a client and the legal defenses and ethical considerations which permit an attorney not to disclose evidence. The author argues that attorneys should accept and hold only that evidence which facilitates their investigation and preparation of a defense, and only for the time necessary to do so. They should then return it to their client with advice about the client's legal obligations.

Note. "Ethics, Law, and Loyalty: The Attorney's Duty to Turn Over Incriminating Physical Evidence." Stanford Law Review 32 (1980), 977-999.

Criticizes a holding by the Alaska Supreme Court that an attorney has an affirmative duty to turn over incriminating physical evidence received from his client. The author suggests procedural methods to balance the attorney's ethical and legal responsibilities by retaining the evidence until it is subpoenaed or otherwise lawfully obtained by the prosecution.

Pye, A. Kenneth. "Role of Counsel in the Suppression of Truth." Duke Law Journal 4 (Oct. 1978), 921-959.

Explores the nature of the legal profession using a hypothetical armed robbery case to illustrate conduct by the defense counsel that ultimately does not serve the public interest.

E. CONFIDENTIALITY

American Business Law Association. Recent Developments in the Law of Confidentiality. Atlanta, GA: American Business Law Association, 1976. 10p. (microfiche)

In Boyd versus U.S. (1886) the Supreme Court introduced what became known as the private papers doctrine of confidentiality which prohibited government action compelling selfincrimination through the defendant's own private papers if such papers were only of evidentiary value. The sum effect of several more recent decisions has been an end to the private papers doctrine. Oral attorney-client communications and documents written under physical or moral compulsion have, however, remained beyond the reach of government and a number of judicial decisions in the area of adult consensual sexual behavior has recognized and extended confidentiality rights.

Armani, Frank H. "The Obligation of Confidentiality." Juris (March 1975), 3-5.

Discusses the ethics of concealing evidence obtained from Robert Garrow by his defense attorney in the famous murder trial. During the trial, Armani was informed about two bodies and did not tell the authorities. He justifies his withholding of evidence by claiming that "no man can serve two masters" and that a lawyer's primary responsibility is to his client. He concludes that a client must be able to talk openly with his attorney, otherwise our concept of a free society will be destroyed.

"Attorney-Client Privilege -- Fixed Rules, Balancing, and Constitutional Entitlement." Harvard Law Review 91 (De 1977), 464-487.

Examines inconsistencies in judicial applications of attorney-client privilege and proposes a model that reflects the privilege's grounding in calculations of social costs and benefits. Three possible nonutilitarian justifications for privilege are considered with a view toward the derivation of a right to privilege, free from utilitarian-balancing. It is argued that individual criminal defendants do have such a right, but that the privilege claims of all other clients must be subject to a rigorous balancing analysis.

Callan, J. Michael, and Harris David. "Professional Responsibility and the Duty of Confidentiality: Disclosure of Client Misconduct in an Adversary System." Rutgers Law Review 29 (1976), 332-396.

Defines legal and ethical principles relevant to the question: When should an attorney voluntarily disclose the past, continuing or intended misconduct of a client? Authors examine relevant principles and develop a framework within which the attorney can evaluate and determine obligations to disclose. They discuss the uncertainty prevailing in this area and the need for clearly defined standards.

Chamberlain, Jeffrey F. "Legal Ethics - Confidentiality and the Case of Garrow's Lawyers." Buffalo Law Review 25:1 (1975), 211-239.

Traces the historical roots of the attorney-client privilege. Discusses an extraordinary New York case in which two attorneys felt bound by their client's privilege toconceal the location of the 2 buried bodies of persons their clients murdered. Concludes that though the privilege may lead to technical violations of the law, its value outweighs that risk.

"Discovery of 'Privileged' Communications." Defense Law Journal 22 (1973), 399-413.

Summarizes recent case law on the subject of privileged communications. A client raised the privilege to bar his accountants from obtaining depositions from his attorneys, who had been retained to defend the client before the IRS for a tax deficiency. The client alleged that the deficiency arose from the negligent preparation of his returns by the accountants. The court held that the accountants were entitled to depositions describing the substance of the presentation made to the tax tribunal. In another case, statements made by a defendant to the employees of her insuror, who was obligated to defend her, were held to be protected by the attorney-client privilege.

Freedman, Monroe H. "'Major Deficiencies' Mar Roles in Lawyer - Client Confidences." Legal Times Washington 4 (10 Aug. 1981), p. 23, col. 1.

Criticizes proposed amendments to the Code of Professional Responsibility arguing that they would effect a radical change in the lawyer-client relationship and violate the 5th and 6th Amendments. The disputed proposals require a lawyer to disclose false testimony evidence, and to inform his client of the limits on confidentiality.

Grace, Roger M. "Invading the Privacy of the Attorney-Client Relationship." Case and Comment 81 (July-August 1976), 46-49.

Discusses judicial attempts to limit the scope of the attorney-client privilege. Grace suggests that this trend is an overreaction to attorney involvement in the Watergate scandal.

Hipler, Harry M. "Turning Point Between Lawyers and Accomplice." Trial 12:5 (1976), 48-50, 61.

Discusses some ethical problems faced by a lawyer whose client arrives for consultation with a weapon which was used in the crime. Hipler discusses the appropriate advice an attorney should give a client under such circumstances and what he should do with physicial evidence that comes into his possession.

Jacobs, Myra R. "Ethical Quandary -- The Extension of Attorney-Client Privilege to Communication of Past Crimes." Case and Comment 81:4 (July-Aug. 1976), 24-28, 30, 3233, 36-39.

Examines development of the principle of privileged attorney-client communications, related constitutional protections, and limitations of the privilege.

Landesman, Bruce M. "Confidentiality and the Lawyer-Clien Relationship.In "Utah Law Review. 1980:4 (1980), 765-786 Reprinted in Ethics and the Legal Profession. eds Frederick A. Elliston and Michael Davis. Buffalo, NY Prometheus, 1984.

Focuses on the differences between the proposed Model Rules of Professional Conduct and the presently enforced Code of Professional Responsibility. Section one discusses the differences in regard to confidentiality in the lawyer-client relationship. Sections two and three address the moral basis, complexity and limits of confidentiality. Section four analyzes the various arguments given for the view that very little, if anything, should be disclosed by the lawyer. The concluding section proposes that the motive for greater disclosure stems from obligations to third parties and the lawyer's own moral autonomy.

O'Neal, F. Hodge, and Stephen R. Thompson. "Vulnerability of Professional-Client Privilege in Shareholder Litigation." Business Lawyer 31 (1976), 1775-1797.

Describes the basis and scope of the attorney-client privilege and its effect upon the responsibilities of corporate counsel where the interests of minority shareholders are asserted in a derivative suit. The author discusses the means of attacking the privilege in shareholder litigation and its intrinsic limitations.

Weissenberger, Glen. "Toward Precision in the Application of the Attorney-Client Privilege For Corporations." Iowa Law Review 65 (1980), 899-930.

Argues that while the attorney-client privilege induces candor in consultation, it does not increase the probability of lawful client behavior. Courts have applied the privilege to corporate clients without fully analyzing its appropriateness in terms of the premises supporting confidentiality. Weissenberger argues that privilege should attach only to communications that would not have been made but for pursuit of legal advice.

F. PERJURY

"Client Fraud and the Lawyer -- An Ethical Analysis." Minnesota Law Review 62:1 (1977), 89-118.

Proposes amending the ABA Code of Professional Responsibility regarding client perjury to impose upon the lawyer who discovers his client's fraud a mandatory duty to disclose the fraud to the injured person. Attorney is sworn not only to represent his client but to promote justice. He must, therefore, insure that his skills are not used to perpetrate a fraud for another person.

Denecke, Arno H. "The Dilemma of the Virtuous Lawyer or When Do You Have to Blow the Whistle on Your Client." Arizona State Law Journal (1979), 245-252.

Examines the ethical obligation of a lawyer to divulge client confidences. Traditionally, confidentiality between lawyer and client is protected at almost all costs. In a civil case involving National Student Marketing Corporation, the court held that attorneys had a duty to inform stockholders of a discrepancy in the financial statement, but did not elaborate on the duties of an attorney in a securities transaction. Criminal law poses the dilemma of confidentiality versus the rights of the accused. The essay discusses two cases to illustrate this conflict: State v. Robinson and Lowery v. Cardwell.

Gordon, Michael D. "The Invention of a Common Law Crime: Perjury and The Elizabethan Courts." American Journal of Legal History 24 (April 1980), 145-170.

Examines the perjury statue of 1563 in an effort to understand the Tudor attitude toward the enactment of statutory law. It has been suggested that during the 16th and 17th Centuries, statutory law was not considered innovative, but more a confirmation of existing common law. The Perjury Statute was an innovative law -- creating a new crime. Gordon seeks to understand how it could be innovative and yet be seen as not innovative by its contemporaries.

Hunter, Muir. False Witness -- The Problem of Perjury -- A Report by Justice. London: Stevens and Sons, 1973.

Examines the lack of prosecution of perjury offenses, remedies for the victims of perjury, the nature of the witness' oath, and the responsibility of lawyers for the evidence given by their witnesses.

Kramer, Victor H. "Clients' Frauds and Their Lawyers' Objections: A Study in Professional Irresponsibility: Georgetown Law Journal 67 (1979), 991-1006.

Traces the history of the proposed provision of the ABA Code of Professional Responsibility which requires disclosure of unrectified client fraud except when it would breach the attorney-client privilege. Kramer author notes that the proposal is rejected by a large percentage of the bar because it would undermine the privilege. He advocates a new disciplinary rule that would require an attorney who was unable to persuade his client to rectify a fraud to withdraw from the representation.

Lawry, Robert P. "Lying, Confidentiality, and the Adversary System of Justice." Utah Law Review 1977 (1977), 653-695.

Discusses a lawyer's ethical duty not to allow a client's perjury to corrupt the legal system. Lawry argues that the source of controversy over this rather clear axiom is a general failure to understand the nature of the adversary system and the balance between the attorney's roles as advocate and officer of the court.

Lefstein, Norman. "The Criminal Defendant Who Proposes Perjury: Rethinking the Defense Lawyer's Dilemma." Hofstra Law Review 6 (1979), 665-692.

Discusses Freedman's view that a criminal defense lawyer must put his client on the stand to testify, even knowing that the client will commit perjury. The American Bar Association's Defense Function Standards propose that a lawyer who knows that a client is intent on perjury should seek to withdraw from the case. Otherwise, the defendant should be asked to make a statement to the trier of fact, and the false testimony should not be argued to the jury. A third possible approach requires the defense attorney to disclose the defendant's intention to the court. Lefstein recommends that the attorney advise the defendant at the outset that his intent to testify falsely is not a privileged communication.

Ostergaard, Joni H. "The Failure of Situation-Oriented Professional Rules to Guide Conduct: Conflicting Responsibilities of the Criminal Defense Attorney Whose Client Commits or Intends to Commit Perjury." Washington Law Review 55 (1979), 211-242.

Demonstrates by means of the example of a perjured client the failure of situation-oriented rules to guide attorney conduct where dual roles as client advocate and officer of the court conflict. Ostergaard proposes system-oriented rules which define the lawyer's role in terms of the overall goals of the legal system. Such rules might allow for separate orientations in different professional contexts such as prosecution and defense.

Plescia, Joseph. The Oath and Perjury in Ancient Greece. Tallahassee, FL: State University Press, 1970.

Traces the historical development of the oath in ancient Greece in the period between Homer and Aristotle and discusses the nature of the various oaths as used primarily by the Athenians. These include public, judicial, international and social oaths. The book's emphasis is on the legal concept of the oath. Specifically, it offers a comprehensive view of the oath with a historical analysis to provide a proper perspective.

"Perjury -- The Forgotten Offense." Journal of Criminal Law and Criminology 65:3 (September 1974), 361-372.

The elements of perjury and reasons for the failure to enforce perjury are examined. Topics discussed include the historical development of perjury as a criminal offense, the effects of perjury, and remedies.

Polster, Dan Aaron. "Dilemma of the Perjurious Defendant -- Resolution, Not Avoidance." Case Western Reserve Law Review 28 (Fall 1977), 3-40.

Assesses proposed solutions to the ethical dilemma confronting the criminal defense lawyer whose client perjures himself, and proposes an alternative solution in which the attorney is required to inform the client at the outset that the attorney will disclose any perjury on the client's part to the court. This solution would provide honesty in the attorney-client relationship while preserving the integrity of the judicial process.

Wilder, Billy, director. The Fortune Cookie. With Walter Matthau and Jack Lemmon. Mirisch Corp., 1966. 125 min.

Comedy-drama in which a dishonest lawyer railroads his brother-in-law, slightly injured while filming a pro football game, into faking injuries and suing several defendants.

• Wolfram, Charles W. "Client Perjury." Southern California Law Review 50 (1977), 809-870.

Discussion of the risks of perjury (both for the perjuror and his counsel), the treatment of client perjury under the Code of Professional Responsibility, the significance of the risk within the context of the adversary system, and the duties of counsel regarding a client who has committed or intends to commit perjury. Wolfram believes that an attorney who doubts his client's honesty should rarely be forced to represent that client.

PART THREE

RELATED MATERIALS

CHAPTER SIX
PHILOSOPHICAL MATERIALS

A. ETHICS

Baier, Kurt. The Moral Point of View. New York: Random House, 1965.

A short and readable introduction to ethics divided into seven chapters. The first discusses different kinds of value judgments and ways to prove them. The second distinguishes deliberating, justifying and explaining. The third provides rules for reasoning: short-term, long-term and other-regarding. Baier distinguishes various social rules in the fourth chapter, especially in religion, law and custom. Chapter five argues against emotivists (like Stevenson) and prescriptivists (like Hare) that moral beliefs can be true or false: moral rules are meant for everyone (universalizable) and must be for the good of everyone alike (utilitarian). Chapter six ties this conception of morality to society and chapter seven explains why we should be moral.

Donagan, Alan. The Theory of Morality. Chicago: University of Chicago Press, 1977.

An attempt to elucidate the common morality passed down in the West as part of our Judeo-Christian heritage. In the first two chapters Donagan discusses various theories of morality, and distinguishes between first order precepts, which determine whether or not an actor is right or wrong and second order precepts that provide a method for assigning blame or praise. Donagan thinks the most fundamental first order precept is, "It is impermissible not to respect every human being as a rational creature.". From this Donagan derives a number of subsidiary first order precepts, which fall into three categories of duties to oneself, to others and to institutions. Donagan analyzes notions like intention, responsibility, and voluntary, in order to arrive at his second order precepts.

Frankena, William K. Ethics. Englewood Cliffs, NJ: Prentice Hall, 1963.

A brief but comprehensive introduction to ethics. The first chapter describes the nature of ethics or moral philosophy. The second focuses on deontological theories: egotists, act and rule. The third deals with two kinds of utilitarianism (act and rule) and discusses their relationship to benevolence, justice, obligation and love. The fourth analyzes the morally good personality. The fifth takes up the hedonistic view that pleasure alone is good in itself, concluding with a discussion of the good life. The final chapter deals with meta-ethics, the analysis of moral discourse and ways of proving moral theories.

Fried, Charles. Right and Wrong. Cambridge, MA: Harvard University Press, 1978.

A discussion of rights and wrongs in two sections and a short final section on the relationship between roles and rights. Fried distinguishes between what is good and what is right: the former is determined by the consequences of an action, the latter by the character of the action itself. He distinguishes positive rights, claims that persons have on society's resources which should be allocated on the basis of fair share, from the more fundamental negative rights which determine what actually counts as a fair share. Fried argues that both rights and duties accrue to persons who have adopted a role, but there is what Fried calls a "discretionary domain," which allows some leeway in the way in which these rights and duties are performed.

Hare, Richard M. The Language of Morals. Oxford: The Clarendon Press, 1952.

An analysis of the meanings of ethical terms, rather than specific issues of right and wrong, divided into three sections. The first examines prescriptive language, not as strong as a command but more of a commendation. The second and central section argues moral language is essentially prescriptive, a recommendation that some action be performed. There is no particularly moral sense of the work "good". It functions to commend the object or action, and secondarily to describe. But the logic of the word "good" requires us to use it consistently.

Harman, Gilbert. The Nature of Morality. New York: Oxford University Press, 1977.

An advanced work in five divisions: the problem with ethics, emotivism, the moral law, reasons and conventions, and oneself and others. Harman argues for a theory based on social convention or custom, which holds that right and wrong are determined by the rules, laws, and mores of a given society at a given time. He emphasizes, however, that this does not make the moral coextensive with the legal, since laws may be passed which violate more fundamental societal principles, such as those expressed in a constitution.

MacIntyre, Alasdair. After Virtue. Notre Dame, IN: University of Notre Dame Press, 1981.

An innovative book that traces attempts to revive the notion of virtue through the emotivists, the Enlightenment and Medievalists to Aristotle and to identify sociological reasons for its neglect. By using insights from ethics, sociology, and history MacIntyre tries to develop a contemporary and justifiable account of virtue. He explains the contemporary confusion in ethics with a fragmentary ethical system divorced from its original framework, namely Ancient Greece. MacIntyre understands virtue to be an excellence in a "practice" or cooperative activity. To avoid the contemporary critique of Aristotelian ethics that it relies on a natural teleological metaphysics, MacIntyre substitutes the notion of a unity of life which involves performing actions with an eye on both one's own past, the future and the social context.

Mackie, John Leslie Ethics. New York: Penguin Books, 1978.

An advanced work in three sections. The first analyzes the meaning of good, the is-ought problem and the universalizability of moral judgements. In the second, Mackie advances his own theory. Although there are no objective moral values, people have various goals. Human well-being is the most common. He discusses the meaning and moral consequences of having such a goal He compares his theory with utilitarian and deontological ones, concluding that his theory is a variety of rule utilitarianism. In the short concluding section Mackie discusses the relations among ethics, psychology, religion and politics, including a section on free will, choice and responsibility.

Rawls, John. A Theory of Justice. Cambridge, MA: Harvard University Press, 1971.

A modern classic that attempts to reconcile utilitarian and deontological theories. Rawls defends a novel theory using a novel approach to justice that asks us to choose principles behind a veil of ignorance so that we do not know what our station in life is. He contends that rational self-interested people would choose three principles of justice: the greatest equal liberty compatible with a like liberty for all; open offices with competition based on merit; and differential rewards attached to these offices provided that they work to the advantage of the least advantaged.

Smart, J. J. C. "Utilitarianism." In Encyclopedia of Philosophy, ed. Paul Edwards (New York: Collier Macmillan Publishing Co.) vol. 8, pp. 206-212.

A simple and brief statement of utilitarianism. Smart defines it as the view that the rightness or wrongness of an action is to be judged solely by its consequences. That particular actions be so judged is known as act utilitarianism; that types of actions or practices be judged is rule utilitarianism. According to universal, utilitarianism, all the consequences must be considered, whereas egoistic utilitarianism considers only those that affect agent the agent. He concludes with some criticisms of utilitarianism. First, there can be no ultimate proof of utilitarianism. This is a criticism to which any positive ethical theory is susceptible. Second, its principles may lead to actions intuitively wrong, for example lying or harming an innocent person. The utilitarian has little choice but to argue our ordinary moral intuitions must be rejected.

Stevenson, C. L. Ethics & Language. New Haven: Yale University Press, 1946.

A major contribution to the meta-ethical discussions which began at the turn of the century with G. E. Moore's Principia Ethica. Stevenson presents a classically emotivist analysis of "good". Its primary function is not to state some fact, but to express the speakers feelings of approval. It also serves to exhort the hearer to approve of the action as well. Thus, as long as there are disagreements in attitude about what people approve or disapprove of, there will be irresolvable moral difference. Thus moral arguments are essentially persuasive or psychological.

B. PROFESSIONAL ETHICS

Baumrin, Bernard and Benjamin Freedman, ed. Moral Responsibility and the Professions. New York: Haven Publications, 1983.

A useful anthology divided into five sections. The first discusses general problems of professional ethics such as the attributes of a profession, the nature of professional ethics, ethical discourse an the philosophy of codes of ethics. The second section provides reading in medicine and law. The third section deals with ethical issues in the sciences, the fourth with politics and the final section with business. An appendix contains several professional codes but there is no bibliography or index.

Bayles, Michael D. Professional Ethics. Belmont, CA: Wadsworth Publishing Co., 1981.

Examines professions from the viewpoint of the average citizen in a liberal society to determine ethical norms. The first chapter discusses the scope of professional ethics and notes significant characteristics of the professions during the last part of the twentieth century. Chapter two addresses the relations between professional and ordinary ethical norms, the justification of professional ethical norms, and the distinctions between various types of norms. Chapters three through six analyze the substantive obligations of professions and professionals, including access to professional services, ethical obligations that arise from accepting a client, obligations of professionals to people who are not their clients, and obligations of professionals to their own professions. The last chapter discusses methods of ensuring that professionals conform to ethical norms, reviewing criteria for admission and self-regulation. Study questions and problems accompany each chapter. A four page selected bibliography is included.

Bennion, F. A. R. Professional Ethics: The Consultant Professions and Their Code. London: Charles Knight & Co., 1969.

Describes the elements of professionalism and discusses the functions of the consulting professions from both the client's and the professional's points of view. Bennion considers the reasons for the development of the professional way of doing business and discusses particular aspects of it: professional organization, means of attracting business and attitudes about advertising, solicitation and fees.

Camenisch, Paul. Grounding Professional Ethics in a Pluralistic Society. New York: Haven Publications, 1983.

A complementary study to Goldman's work that seeks to establish a basis for professional ethics in a pluralistic society. Chapter one defines the profession and chapter two the meanings of professionalism. Chapter three characterizes professions as moral communities and analyzes the relations between professional and social standards. Chapter four takes up the challenge to professional ethics posed by pluralism and argues for a lived moral consensus. Chapter five uses this consensus to deal with promises, roles and gifts. Chapter six concludes by outlining the shape of professional ethics, using the relationship between clients and professionals and the problem of access to professional services as two illustrations.

Dansereau, H. R. "Unethical Behavior: Professional Deviance." In Deviance in Business and The Professions. eds. John M. Johnson and Jack D. Douglas. Philadelphia: J.B. Lippincott, 1978.

Distinguishes professional work from lay occupations noting that professional work is based on a systematic knowledge acquired through extensive training and that professionals adhere to professional norms. Dansereau states that blue-collar and semi-professional workers are unlikely to have opportunities to engage in violations typical of professional unethical conduct. He discusses the nature and rationale of unethical behavior.

Elliston, Frederick A. "Professionalism and Professional Ethics." Paper presented at the American Society of Public Administrators in Honolulu, Hawaii: March 25, 1982.

Argues that in order to be a professional one must be a moral philosopher. The first section discusses moral philosophy and recent applied philosophy. The second describes work currently done in professional ethics. The third defines a profession. The fourth and main section shows what moral philosophy has to contribute to professionalization in terms of moral consciousness raising, the clarification of moral terms, the evaluation of moral arguments and the search for moral truths. The fifth and final section identifies two routes towards greater professionalism: that philosophers become more versed in the professions, or that professionals become more versed in philosophy.

"Ethics in America -- Norms and Deviations." Annals of the American Academy of Political and Social Science. 363 (Jan. 1966), entire.

A collection of articles on the norms and deviations of ethics in American government, business, and the professions. Subjects range from whether the code of ethics in public life should be absolute or relative, to judicial ethics, to unethical behavior in government. Legal delays is also represented.

Freedman, Benjamin. "A Meta-Ethics for Professional Morality." Ethics 89 (Oct. 1978), 1-19.

Argues that what is moral for one as a professional may conflict with the requirements of ordinary morality. This conflict is similar to, but stronger than, those conflicts which can be generated by acquired moralities in general, such as promise-keeping. Standard deontological and act-utilitarian explanations are inadequate to explain this conflict. A theory is constructed, similar to Freedman's interpretation of Lon Fuller's theory of internal morality of law but dignificantly different from role-utilitarianism.

Freedman, Benjamin. "What Really Makes Professional Morality Different: Response to Martin." Ethics 91 (1981), 626-630.

Distinguishes ordinary morality from professional morality, which may demand acts of forebearance which would be immoral in other contexts. Ordinary morality emanates from the rule-free, pure human condition while professional morality is based upon the functional nature of the professional role.

Goldman, Alan H. The Moral Foundations of Professional Ethics. Totowa, NJ: Rowman and Littlefield, 1980.

Explores the degree to which various professional roles

require special moral principles to guide their conduct. To what extent do professionals have rights or obligations to ignore normally relevant considerations in acting in official capacities? Begins from a moral framework defined in terms of rights and considers arguments deriving from the institutional goals of each profession. These include zealous advocacy for lawyers, national interest for politicians, optimal health care for doctors, and profit for business managers.

Kipnis, Kenneth. "Professional Responsibility and the Responsibility of Professions." Profits and Professions ed. Wade L. Robison, Michael S. Pritchard and Joseph Ellin (New York: Humana Press, 1983, pp. 9-22.

Discusses whether there is justification for special standards for the conduct of members of a profession, and whether it is possible to delineate the proper dimensions of these standards and to assess the magnitude of the claim they have on professionals. The nature of responsibility, the reasons why professions have responsibilities and the relation between the responsibility of a profession and that of its members are discussed as a means of approaching the philosophical issues in professional ethics.

Kipnis, Kenneth, ed. Ethics in the Professions: An Anthology. Belmont, CA: Wadsworth Publishing Co. 1984.

A comprehensive anthology of readings in the area of professional ethics that brings together various published and unpublished materials.

Larson, M. S. The Rise of Professionalism: A Sociological Analysis. Berkeley: University of California Press, 1977.

An important book on professions. Larson has attempted to summarize its central ideas in a review essay in The British Journal of Law and Society 6 (1979), 82-98.

C. THE PHILOSOPHY OF LAW

Albrecht, Adalbert, trans. Philosophy of Law, by Josef Kohler. New York: Augustus M. Kelley, 1969.

A treatise which discusses the philosophy of law, its significance, its role in the development of culture and its function in achieving legal order and peaceable regulation. Separate sections treat the law of persons, property, the state and international relations.

Bingham, Joseph Walter, et al. My Philosophy of Law: Credos of Sixteen American Scholars. Boston, MA: Boston Law Book, 1941.

The preface calls this "a buffet feast of ideas" to which the philosopher, who thinks too little of law, and the lawyer, who ponders too little in philosophy, might well be summoned with promise of delight and profit. These essays illustrate the editors' view that legal philosophers are more in agreement than is evident form their points of disagreement.

Bishin, William R. and C. D. Stone. Law, Language and Ethics. Mineola, NY: Foundation Press, 1972.

Compendious collection of materials on many aspects of law and ethics, including the interaction with and limitations placed on these disciplines by language. Contains a sizeable bibliography.

Burns, Jeremy H., gen. ed. The Collected Works of Jeremy Bentham. London: Athline Press, 1970.

Jeremy Bentham (1748-1832) was a leader of the British Utilitarian reformers who became known as the Philosophical Radicals. His works on law, philosophy, social policy, religion and penology along with his collected correspondence are published in this edition of 38 volumes. Works cover such topics as principles of legislation, penology and criminal law, civil law, civil law, constitutional law and law reform.

Cairns, Huntington. Legal Philosophy from Plato to Hegel. Baltimore: John Hopkins Press, 1949.

Attempts to argue that modern jurisprudence is in its essentials a prolongation of the great philosophical systems. Contains 15 chapters on Plato, Aristotle, Cicero, Aquinas, Bacon, Hobbes, Spinoza, Leibniz, Locke, Hume, Kant, Fichte and Hegel. He takes jurisprudence's primary objective to be to understand the function of law in society. For Cairns law serves to sustain and stabilize the social fabric.

Davis, Philip E., ed. Moral Duty and Legal Responsibility. A Philosophical - Legal Casebook. Reprint of 1966 edition. New York: Meredith Publishing Co., 1981.

Contains articles on the ethical bases of assigning rights and duties, allowing justifications and defenses, allowing causes of action, adopting legal norms and setting the limits of advocacy.

Dworkin, Ronald. Taking Rights Seriously. Cambridge, MA: Harvard University Press, 1977.

A noted positivist legal scholar presents his theory of rights and applied it to contemporary issues.

De Gregorio, Cosimo. Treatise on Ethics at Law. Boston, MA: Meador, 1948.

Outlines the duty of the lawyer in a variety of professional roles including officer of the court, counsel for the indigent, representative of the accused, member of an honorable profession, and seeker of truth.

Feinberg, Joel and Hyman Gross, ed. Philosophy of Law. Belmon, CA: Wadsworth Publishing Co., 1975.

A basic text for philosophy of law courses, divided into five sections: law, liberty, justice, responsibility and punishment. The readings include court cases, and historical and contemporary writings by philosophers and legal scholars. A brief introduction is provided at the beginning of each section, and a useful set of further readings at the end.

Friedrich, Carl J. The Philosophy of Law in Historical Perspective. 2nd ed. Chicago: University of Chicago Press, 1963.

Discusses the current problems of the philosophy of law, within the framework of its history. Various philosophical views of the nature of law are presented in chronological order from the Old Testament through relativism, formalism and skepticism. Friedrich believes an historical perspective is important because the intellectual history of thinking about law exhibits design and successive philosophies of law embody progressive insights.

Fuller, Lon L. The Morality of Law. New Haven, CT: Yale University Press, 1964.

Reprint of lectures delivered at the Yale Law School in 1963. Two moralities are described: the morality of duty and the morality of aspiration. Fuller describes the concept of law in the light of the law's neutral internal morality toward substantive aims.

Fuller, Lon L. "Positivism and Fidelity to Law - A Reply to Professor Hart." Harvard Law Review 71 (1958), 630-672.

Criticizes Hart for ignoring the internal morality of order necessary for the creation of all law. It is not a question of distinguishing law from morality, but of recognizing that there is order and good order. Statutory interpretation is discussed as a means of achieving good order.

Golding, Martin P. Philosophy of Law. Englewood Cliffs, NJ: Prentice-Hall, 1975.

Discusses the nature of law and its authority, its relation to morality, its limits, theories of punishment, and dispute settlement. Includes a topical bibliography.

Golding, Martin P. Legal Reasoning. New York: Alfred A. Knopf, 1984.

A short work, intended as a text, that describes and analyzes judicial decisionmaking not from a psychological but logical and philosophical standpoint. Golding distinguishes the process of discovery from justification and explanation. He provides examples of reasoned judicial decisions and examines the types of arguments employed, especially the appeal to precedent and the argument by anology. In addition to actual cases Golding provides a useful bibliographic essay.

Grey, Thomas. The Legal Enforcement of Morality. New York: Random House, 1980.

Consists of an introductory essay and legal texts on three issues: the enforcement of sexual morality, the treatment of human remains and the duties of potential rescuers. Grey shows how philosophical problems differ from classroom hypotheticals when they are confronted in a legal setting. He illustrates this point using material from statutes, regulations, judicial opinions, and law review commentaries. Grey reviews the Hart-Devlin debate over the legitimacy of prohibiting homosexual acts. He places the challenging problem of how to treat dead bodies in the context of the debate over morals enforcement, and discusses the Good Samaritan as an issue concerning the propriety of the legal enforcement of moral duties.

Gross, Hyman. A Theory of Criminal Justice. New York: Oxford University Press, 1979.

Attempts to develop a theory of the nature and scope of the criminal law divided into 10 chapters. Chapter one treats the criminal justice system as social criticism, moral criticism, social defense or correction. Chapter two discusses criminal acts in terms of bodily movement plus intention, acts and their consequences and circumstances, and the difference between voluntary and involuntary acts. Chapter three analyzes culpability in terms of intention and motive. Chapter four deals with harms and the punishment of attempted harms. Chapters five, six and seven deal with exculpation in terms of mistaken beliefs, causation, ignorance, compulsion and mental abnormalities. Chapter eight examines the rationale for excuses and the limits of a doctrine of strict liability. Chapter nine develops a theory of punishment called "anti-impunity": the law must threatened punishment in order to keep the community as a whole law-abiding and peaceable. In the final chapter Gross applies his theory of negligence, attempts, sentencing and liability.

Hacker, P. M. S. "Definition in Jurisprudence." Philadelphia Quarterly 19 (Oct. 1969), 343-347.

Attempts to refute the claim that fundamental legal concepts require unique methods of definition. Bentham claimed they cannot be defined by genus and differentia, but only by paraphrasis. In his inaugural lecture Hart revived Bentham's theory regarding the definition of claim-rights and suggested a method of truth-conditional definition of a sentential formula containing "claim-right." Six arguments show that the Benthamite-Hartian claim rests upon inadequate grounds. Hart's definition is examined. The second part of his definition is either mistaken or redundant. The first part is transformable without loss into the traditional mode of definition.

Hacker, P. M. S., and J. Raz, eds. Law, Morality, and Society -- Essays in Honour of H. L. A. Hart. New York, Oxford University Press, 1977.

A collection of essays with themes in jurisprudence, ethics, and social theory. Topics include Hart's philosophy of law, the phenomenon of law, naive instrumentalism and the law, positivism, adjudication, democracy, the House of Lords and the rules of precedent, intention and 'mens rea' (guilty mind) in murder, the grounds of responsibility, rights in legislation, justice between generations, and harm and self-interest. A bibliography of H. L. A. Hart is included.

Harding, Arthur L., ed. Origins of the Natural Law Tradition. Dallas: Southern Methodist University, 1954.

Collection of four essays that describe four major theories of natural law. Theories chosen are those developed in the works of Cicero, Aquinas, Richard Hooker and Herbert Spencer. All four conceive of natural law as a manifestation of universal order.

Hart, H. L. A. "Positivism and the Separation of Law and Morals." Harvard Law Review 71 (1958), 593-629.

Defends the Positivist school of jurisprudence from criticism against its insistence on distinguishing the law that is from the law that ought to be and considers the merits of the distinction.

Kelsen, Hans. Essay in Legal and Moral Philosophy, translated by Peter Heath. Boston: D. Reidel, 1973.

A collection of essays on justice, natural law, religion, law and morality, law and logic, value relativism and the logic of norms. Kelsen's conception of legal science, the Pure Theory of Law, is a unifying theme described in the introduction as a theory which ignores, though it does not deny, the law's connection with the facts of psychology, sociology, morals and politics. It insists emphatically on purity in avoidance of any syncretism of methods, "which obscures the essential character of legal science and erases the boundaries set for it by the nature of its subject-matter."

Kipnis, Kenneth. *Philosophical Issues in Law: Cases and Materials*. Englewood Cliffs, NJ: Prentice Hall, 1977.

A comprehenisvei anthology of materials drawn from law and philosophy for use in legal philosophy courses.

King, J. Charles and James A. McGilvray, ed. *Political and Social Philosophy*. New York: McGraw Hill, 1973.

An anthology of readings in three parts. The first contains excerpts from writings of traditional political theorists from Plato to Kropotkin. The second provides selections from contemporary writers on law, justice, liberty, the public interest, morals, punishment and revolution. The third addresses more popular concerns such as civil disobedience, war, poverty and politics.

Leff, Arthur Allen. "Unspeakable Ethics, Unnatural Law." *Duke Law Journal* 1979 (1979), 1229-1249.

Offers to prove that there can be no normative system based on anything but human will. Leff discusses the consequences of this reasoning as evident in legal scholarship, and how it shapes attitudes toward constitutional interpretation.

Martin, Michael. "Roscoe Pound's Philosophy of Law." *Arch. Phil. Law. Soc. Phil.* 51 (1965), 37-55.

Three crucial aspects of Roscoe Pound's philosophy of law are examined critically: the goal he attributes to a legal system, his philosophy of the history of law and his theory of judicial interpretation. Martin shows that the goal Pound attributes to a legal system is unacceptable from a moral point of view, that his theory of legal history rests on a dubious theory of historical truth, and that his theory of judicial interpretation is based on a problematic metaphysics and epistemology.

Morawetz, Thomas A. *The Philosophy of Law, An Introduction*. New York: Macmillan, 1980.

An introductory text divided into four chapters: Philosophy and the Concept of Law, Judicial Decisions, Morality and Legislation, and Responsibility and Punishment. Morawetz examines two theoretical approaches to law: first, the utilitarian emphasis on benefits to citizens; and second, the deontological or rights theorists' emphasis on the independence of individuals from unwarranted governmental interference.

Morris, Clarence, ed. *The Great Legal Philosophers*. Philadelphia: University of Pennsylvania Press, 1959.

A comprehensive selection of writings on jurisprudence by 22 philosophers with brief introductions to each. Excerpts are taken from works by Aristotle, Cicero, Aquinas, Grotius, Hobbes, Locke, Mill, Ihering, Holmes, Ehrlich, Dabin, Dewey, Cardozo and Pound. Also contains a lengthy topical index.

Packer, Herbert. *The Limits of the Criminal Sanction*. Stanford: Stanford University Press, 1968.

A modern classic on the problem of trying to control anti-social behavior by imposing a sanction on those found guilty of violating criminal statutes. The first part is an extended essay on the nature of the criminal sanction or punishment. Part two explores the tension between the crime control and due process models of criminal justiace administration. The third and concluding part argues on utilitarian grounds that the criminal sanction is overused and ought to be curtailed.

Posner, Richard A. "Lawyers as Philosophers: Ackerman and Others." Review of *Social Justice in the Liberal State*, by Bruce Ackerman. *American Bar Foundation Research Journal* 1981 (1981), 231-249.

Criticizes Ackerman's tendency to give terms such as liberalism and equality new meanings from which he attempts to deduce policy recommendations. Posner notes a tendency among legal scholars to seek insights usable in legal studies from political and moral philosophy. Ackerman departs from this by discussing philosophy alone. He supports this departure but notes that some characteristics of legal reasoning, such as the use of fictions, are inappropriate and misleading when adapted to political philosophy.

Richards, David A. J. *The Moral Criticism of Law*. Encino, CA: Dickinson Publishing, 1977.

An introduction to the philosophy of law, using moral philosophy as a basis for a philosophical examination of the values in constitutional law. Richards discusses natural law and legal positivism, outlining the current debate on both. The topics pursued include obscenity and sexual conduct; justice and the constitutionality of school financing; sex-based discrimination; responsibility in criminal law; and a comparison between moral and constitutional theories of just punishment.

Sawer, Geoffrey. Law in Society. Oxford: Clarendon Press, 1965.

Summarizes some problems concerning the social history and relations of law with illustrations from different social and legal systems. Sawer discusses law in primitive societies and considers social and legal evolution, legal institutions such as courts, bench and bar, and methods of social control.

Sayre, Paul. Philosophy of Law. Iowa City: State University of Iowa, 1954.

Discusses the nature and interrelation of values and norms in the making and application of law. Sayre notes the limitations of both and describes the process of balancing their influence in making legal decisions to achieve justice.

Stumpf, Samuel Enoch. Morality and the Law. Nashville, TN: Vanderbilt University Press, 1966.

Challenges the modern concept of law as morally neutral by exploring the relationship of law and morality in five different ways, each representing a major theory of law. Those theories are that the law is what the courts do in fact; that law is the will of the economically dominant class; that law is the command of the sovereign; international law; and natural law. Stumpf adheres to Thomas Hobbes' theory of natural law and agrees with Hobbes that the legal order rests upon moral order.

Summers, Robert S., ed. Essays in Legal Philosophy. Berkeley: University of California Press, 1968.

A collection of essays on the concept of legal liberty, intention and purpose in law, methods of dispute resolution, morality and the criminal law, legislation and legislative intent, and the decision-making of the Supreme Court.

Summers, Robert S., ed. More Essays in Legal Philosophy: General Assessments of Legal Philosophies. Berkeley: University of California Press, 1971.

This collection of essays describes various schools of legal philosophy. Scholars considered are Bentham, Pound, Kelsen, Fuller and Hart.

Wasserstrom, Richard A. The Judicial Decision. Stanford, CA: Stanford University Press, 1961.

Posits that reason or logic ought to have a function in judicial decision-making through implementation of a two-level procedure of justification. First, a decision must be shown to be formally deducible from some legal rule. Second, the rule upon which its justification depends must be desirable and defensible. The book is divided into eight chapters and contains a four-page alphabetical bibliography.

Weinreb, Lloyd L. "Law as Order." Harvard Law Review 95 (1978), 909-959.

Analyzes and criticizes Ronald Dworkin's attack on legal positivism's assertion that law and morality are not fundamentally or necessarily connected. Natural law theorists hold the opposite notion. Dworkin argues that positivism confuses normative and descriptive discourse. Weinreb argues that Dworkin misinterprets the essential doctrines of legal positivism, which make the normative character of law central to its argument against natural law. Law and morals are separate normative systems. Nonetheless, he argues that the conceptual framework of our experience does not unequivocally separate the descriptive and the normative, and therefore a case for some form of natural law can still be made.

Wooton, Barbara. Crime and Penal Policy. Boston, MA: George Allen and Unwin, 1978.

Contains the personal reflections of a London magistrate during her more than 50 years on the bench, divided into two parts. In the first, after a brief description of her own career, Wooton discusses reaching a verdict, the function of sentencing, limitations on the sentencing function, the personnel of the courts, custodial and non-custodial sentences. In the second part she deals with some special problems for the courts:

murder, young offenders, drugs and drunks, motorists and the mentally abnormal offenders. Noting a marked increase in the number of crimes over the past 50 years, she derides the effort to identify the causes of crimes, but recommends studying its origins especially in noxious social habits. She defends incarceration in terms of public protection and criticizes parole for endangering it.

CHAPTER SEVEN
OTHER MATERIALS

A. POPULAR BOOKS

Abt, Lawrence E. and Irving R. Stuart, eds. Social Psychology and Discretionary Law. New York: Van Nostrand Reinhold Company, 1979.

Collection of articles reviewing the study and functions of discretion in various legal contexts. Includes judges, prosecutors, police and defense counsel.

Bazelon, David T. "Views from a Law Office Window." In Nothing But a Fine Tooth Comb: Essays in Social Criticism, 1944-1969. New York: Simon and Schuster, 1969, 228-332.

Contains five book reviews relevant to the legal profession: My Life in Court by Louis Nizer; Justice on Trial: The Case of Louis D. Brandeis by A.L. Todd; Powers of Attorney by Louis Auchincloss; The Wall Street Lawyer by Erwin D. Smigel; and The Lawyers by Martin Meyer. Also included are two articles discussing lawyers as "generalists" and the lawyer-client relationship.

Berman, Harold J., ed. Talks on American Law. New York: Vintage, 1961.

Contains a series of broadcasts prepared for the Voice of America for transmission worldwide. The authors were members of the Harvard Law faculty. Topics include the history of American law, the functions of the judge, counsel and jury, the rights of the accused and racial minorities, constitutional rights of citizens, the function of the Supreme Court and administrative, labor, commercial and property law. Contains chapters on the legal profession and legal education.

Bloomfield, Maxwell. Law & Lawyers in American Popular Culture. New York: McGraw-Hill, 1982.

Discusses popular images of the lawyer, showing how contemporary values and attitudes toward the law are reflected in fiction. Bloomfield focuses on two historical periods: antebellum America and the Progressive era. He examines fictional works which were not always literary classics, but exposed particular legal mores.

Dow, Paul E. *Discretionary Justice*. Cambridge, MA: Ballinger Publishing Company, 1981.

Contends due process and the legal rights granted defendants are thwarted by the very system that purports to defend them. Dow suggests that every major legal institution metes out justice with discretion rather than due process. He demonstrates how police, judges, attorneys and juries practice discretionary justice: they protect the rights of the defendant only after satisfying complex bureaucratic, social, and political imperatives. Dow concludes they usually lack standards and often reflect corruption, prejudice or caprice.

Evan, William M., ed. *Law and Sociology: Exploratory Essays.* New York: Free Press of Glencoe, 1962.

A collection of essays addressing the growing realization that law may not continue as a self-sufficient discipline in view of the demands upon it to produce informed social change. The articles concentrate on the possibilities of interaction between law and sociology.

James, Howard. *Crisis in the Courts*. New York: David McKay, 1968.

The extent of case backlog, the political spoils system, the incompetency of many state court judges and existing discrimination against the poor are revealed in this critique of the judicial system. The need for reform is seen in municipal and minor courts, judges and lawyers, the adversary system, police procedures, bail, the right to counsel, juries and the role of the citizen. Numerous case studies are offered.

Patterson, L. Ray and Elliott E. Cheatham. *The Profession of Law*. Mineola, NY: Foundation Press, 1971.

Discusses various aspects of the legal profession including its history, professional standards, the lawyer's function in private, legislative and administrative practice, their roles as judges and counselors to clients. Describes the structure of the organized profession and the methods generally employed in providing legal services.

Siegel, Edward. How to Avoid Lawyers: A Legal Guide for Laymen. New York: Information, Inc., 1969.

A plain language discussion of various decisions faced by people of moderate means. Siegel offers guidance in deciding whether they need an attorney, where to find one and how to choose one in various situations including personal injury, real estate transactions, divorce, wills, business ventures, debts and bankruptcy, condemnation, and involvement in legal proceedings.

B. HISTORICAL MATERIALS

Armstrong, Walter P. "Century of Legal Ethics." American Bar Association Journal 64 (July 1978), 1063-1072.

Traces the history of the American Bar Association's work in legal ethics. The first code of professional ethics was adopted in Alabama in 1887, based largely on a series of lectures given by Judge George Sharswood. In 1908, the American Bar Association adopted the Canons of Professional Ethics and in 1924 it adopted the Canons of Judicial Ethics. Henry Drinker, Chairman of the Committee of Professional Ethics, marked the beginning of a new era. From 1959 to 1969, the Committee published all informal opinions. The final draft of the Code was adopted in 1969. Basically the Code differed from the Canons in form only. It was divided into the canons, ethical considerations, and disciplinary rules.

Bloomfield, Maxwell. American Lawyers in a Changing Society, 1776-1876. Cambridge, MA: Harvard University Press, 1976.

Nine wide ranging essays on individual lawyers and their interaction with law and society during the first century of American independence. Individual essays recount the responses of legal practitioners to major social crises such as the American Revolution, the slavery debates, and urban riots. Bloomfield explores broader themes and movements such as the codification controversy of the 1820's and the image of the legal profession in ante-bellum literature.

Chroust, Anton-Hermann. "The American Legal Profession - Its Agony and Ecstasy (1776-1840)." Notre Dame Lawyer 46 (1971), 487-525.

Describes the history of the bar in the United States during a period when the profession was in great disfavor with the public. Chroust covers the aftermath of the Revolution, when the profession was perceived as an English institution, through the Jacksonian Era when it was perceived as undemocratic.

Chroust, Anton-Hermann. The Rise of the Legal Professional in America. (2 vols.). Norman: University of Oklahoma Press, 1965.

Volume I describes the history of the legal profession in America during the colonial period. Chroust concludes that on the eve of the Revolution most of the colonies had a trained and capable native bar which was already highly influential in politics. Volume II covers the period from the Revolution to developments in the 1840s'. It describes the effects of the Revolution on the professions' fortunes, the beginnings of bar associations, formal legal education, and legislative and judicial attempts to control admission and practices of the bar.

Cohen, Herman. "The Origins of the English Bar." Law Quarterly Review 30 (1914), 464-480.

Traces the descent of the English bar from the decline of the Roman Empire through periods of Frankish and Germanic influences. Discussion culminates in a description of the evolution of the sergeant-at-law.

Fetner, Gerald. "Public Power and Professional Responsibility: Julius Henry Cohen and the Origins of the Public Authority." American Journal of Legal History 21 (1977), 15-39.

Describes lawyers' participation in government efforts at social engineering from the turn of the century through the New Deal. The public authority was a product of this period and was designed to have the power of government without the strife of partisan control. Lawyers developed a new role as the initiators of public policy. He concludes that this new role never materialized because of a conflict between the public and private aspects of professional responsibility thatprevented the development of a consistent policy of public service.

Hazard, Geoffrey C. "An Historical Perspective on the Attorney-Client Privilege." California Law Review 66 (1978), 1061-1091.

Outlines the scope of the modern attorney-client privilege, discusses its rationale, its historical development and speculates upon the probable effect of imposing limits upon it. Hazard summarizes his description of the early English and American cases by suggesting that they provide little guidance for a modern reassessment of the kinds of secrets a lawyer ought to be able to keep. They merely indicate that the problem has always been a difficult one.

Holmes, Oliver W. "The Path of the Law." Harvard Law Review 10 (1897), 457-478.

The distinction between Law and morals is made only for the purpose of examining and understanding the law. Holmes regards law as the history of moral development of the race. He describes the roles of logic and tradition in the development and study of law.

Horwitz, Morton J. "The Conservative Tradition in the Writing of American Legal History." American Journal of Legal History 17 (1973), 275-294.

Argues that the writing of American legal history, a task almost totally performed by lawyers, has long been an occupation thoroughly imbued with a profoundly conservative ideology. Horwitz uses passages from works by Roscoe Pound to illustrate three basic conservative themes in legal historical writing: 1) the triumph of the common law over anglo-philic post-revolutionary reformers and later codifiers like Field; 2) the excellence of the profession during periods when the criteria for admission were stringent; and 3) the rejection of any theory of legal development founded upon economic conditions during the period of change.

Kirk, Harry. Portrait of a Profession: A History of the Solicitors' Profession, 1100 to the Present Day. London: Oyez, 1976.

Describes the history and development of the English solicitors. Kirk discusses the organization of theprofession, educational requirements, conduct and discipline, its functions, relations with the trial bar, status and reputation.

Kogan, Herman. The First Century: The Chicago Bar Association 1874-1974. Chicago: Rand McNally, 1974.

History of the Chicago Bar Association published on its centennial.

Papke, David R. "The Lawyer's Responsibilities: An Historical View." In Ethics and the Legal Profession eds. Frederick A. Elliston and Michael Davis. Buffalo, NY: Prometheus, 1984.

Traces the development of the profession, its social practices and self-impressions beginning with traditional colonial communities up to modern bureaucratic society. Throughout, Papke says, the legal profession has commented upon and directed lawyers' conduct. The stage was set for contemporary discussions of professional ethics by discussions of the lawyer's ethical responsibility to clients, social groups and the whole society.

Pound, Roscoe. The Lawyer from Antiquity to Modern Times. St. Paul, MN: West Publishing Co., 1953.

Describes the historical origins and development of the legal profession and its variants in Western societies, concentrating on the history of the English and American professions and the development of American bar associations.

Pound, Roscoe. "Mechanical Jurisprudence." Columbia Law Journal 8 (1908), 605-623.

A classic essay which points out two dangers of a scientific (mechanical) legal system; first, the effect on the public and second, on the courts and lawyers. Pound fears artificiality in the law could become an end in itself and justice would be overlooked.

Schudson, Michael. "Public, Private, and Professional Lives: The Correspondence of David Dudley Field and Samuel Bowles." American Journal of Legal History 3 (1977), 191-211.

Traces the development of the ethics of legal professionalism in the late 19th century through correspondence between David Dudley Field and Samuel Bowles, a critic of Field's relations with the owners of the Erie Railroad. Field defended his position.

Sharswood, George. An Essay on Professional Ethics. 5th ed. (Reprint of 1844 ed.) Philadelphia, PA: T. & J. W. Johnson & Co., 1930.

A seminal work on the subject of professional ethics. Discusses ethical implications of legislation, constitutions, stare decisis, jurisprudence, duties of lawyers to clients, the profession and the courts, compensation and contingent fees. Sharswood provides legal biographies of Sir William Jones and John Marshall.

Smith, Len Young. "Abraham Lincoln as a Bar Examiner." The Bar Examiner 51:3 (August 1982), 35-37.

An historical narrative about committees charged with overseeing admissions to the Illinois Bar beginning in 1819, including 1836 when Lincoln was certified by the then standing committee, to be of good moral character, and up to 1858, when he was made a board examiner.

Stone, Harlan. "The Public Influence of the Bar." Harvard Law Review 48 (1934), 1-14.

Discusses the history of social change in the United States and the changing role of the bar. Stone calls upon members of the bar to be aware of the responsibilities imposed on them by an influential social and political role.

Wilkin, Robert N. The Spirit of the Legal Profession. New Haven: Yale University Press, 1938.

Discusses the historical high points in the development of the legal profession in ancient Rome, England and the United States. Wilkin praises the profession for its dedication to justice and the Constitution, and exhorts it to carry its high ideals into the Industrial Age.

C. BIBLIOGRAPHIC MATERIALS

Abel, Richard L. "The Sociology of American Lawyers: A Bibliographic Guide." Law and Policy Quarterly 2:3 (July 1980), 335-392.

Arnesen, Nancy, ed. Plea Negotiation: A Selected Bibliography. Washington, DC: U.S. Government Printing Office, May, 1980.

Auerbach, Jerold S. Unequal Justice: Lawyers and Social Change in Modern America. New York: Oxford University Press, 1976, pp. 368-380.

Bayles, Michael D. Professional Ethics. Belmont, CA: Wadsworth Publishing Co., 1981, pp. 152-156.

Blumberg, Abraham S., ed. The Scales of Justice. Newark, NJ: Transaction Books, 1970, pp. 177-188.

Bowie, Norman E. and Frederick A. Elliston, eds. Ethics, Public Policy and Criminal Justice. Cambridge, MA: Oelgeschlager, Gunn and Hain, Inc., 1982, pp. 472-475.

Bowman, James S., Frederick A. Elliston and Paula Lockhart. Professional Dissent: An Annotated Bibliography and Resource Guide. New York: Garland Publishing Co., 1983, pp. 145-160.

Cain, A. A., J. Fisher, N. Arneson, and T. Schrinel. Plea Negotiation -- A Selected Bibliography. Rockville, MD: National Criminal Justice Reference Service, 1980.

Fuchs, A. E. Ethics and the Law, Final Narrative Report, College of William and Mary, Department of Philosophy. Williamsburg, VA: Grant EN-31843-78-0864.

Gorovitz, Samuel and Bruce Miller. Professional Responsibility in the Law, A Curriculum Report from the Institute on Law and Ethics. Williamstown, MA: Council for Philosophical Studies, Summer 1977, pp. 42-46.

Kelly, Michael J. Legal Ethics and Legal Education, The Teaching of Ethics II. Hastings-on-the-Hudson, NY: The Institute of Society, Ethics and Life Sciences, 1980, pp. 55-69.

Klein, Fannie J. National Conference on the Judiciary, an Annotated Bibliography. New York: New York University Institute of Judicial Administration, 1971.

Lefcourt, Robert, ed. Law Against the People. New York: Random House, 1971, pp. 348-371.

Markowitz, Joseph C. Plea Bargaining: An Annotated Bibliography. Chicago, IL: American Journal of Social Sciences, 1978.

Maru, Olavi. Research on the Legal Profession: A Review of Work of Work Done. Chicago, IL: American Bar Foundation, 1985.

Mathews, Robert E. Problems Illustrative of the Responsibilities of Members of the Legal Profession. 2nd revised ed. New York: Council For Legal Education and Professional Responsibility, 1968, xii-xiv.

Mellinkoff, David. The Conscience of a Lawyer. St.Paul, MN: West Publishing Co., 1977, pp. 275-293.

Van Schaick, Jane and Katherine M. Sampson. Selected Literature on Judicial Conduct and Disability: An Annotated Bibliography. Chicago, IL: American Judicature Society, 1983.

Wasserstrom, Richard A. The Judicial Decision. Stanford University Press, 1961, pp. 191-194.

Weckstein, Donald T., ed. Education in the Professional Responsibilities of the Lawyer. The Proceedings of the National Conference, Boulder, CO: University of Colorado, June 10-13 1968, pp. 359-401.

Zemans, Frances K. and Victor G. Rosenblum. The Making of a Public Profession. Chicago, IL: American Bar Foundation, 1981, pp. 235-247.

BAR ASSOCIATION ADDRESSES

BAR ASSOCIATION ADDRESSES

Alabama State Bar
Post Office Box 671
Montgomery, Alabama 36101
(205) 269-1515
Reginald T. Hamner

Alaska Bar Association
Post Office Box 279
Anchorage, Alaska 99510
(907) 272-7469
Randall P. Burns

American Bar Association
National Center for Professional Responsibility
33 W. Monroe St.
Chicago, Illinois 60606
(312) 621-9250

State Bar of Arizona
Suite 858
234 North Central
Phoenix, Arizona 85004
(602) 252-4804
Eldon L. Husted

Arkansas Bar Association
400 West Markham
Little Rock, Arkansas 72201
(501) 375-4605
C.E. Ransick

State Bar of California
555 Franklin Street
San Francisco, California 94102
(415) 561-8200
Richard B. Morris

Colorado Bar Association
200 West 14th Avenue
Denver, Colorado 80204
(303) 629-6873
William B. Miller

Connecticut Bar Association
15 Lewis Street
Hartford, Connecticut 06103
(203) 249-9141
Daniel Hovey

Delaware Bar Association
25 Public Building
Wilmington, Delaware 19801
(302) 658-5278
Charles R. Harris

District of Columbia Bar
8th Floor
1426 H Street, N.W.
Washington, D.C. 20005
(202) 638-1500
J. David Ellwanger

Bar Association of the District of Columbia
Suite 300
1819 H Street, N.W.
Washington, D.C. 20006
(202) 223-1480
Marie J. Rivera

The Florida Bar
The Florida Bar Center
Tallahassee, Florida 32304
(904) 222-5286
John F. Harkness, Jr.

State Bar of Georgia
11th Floor
84 Peachtree Street
Atlanta, Georgia 30303
(404) 522-6255
Wm. B. Spann, Jr.

Hawaii State Bar Association
Post Office Box 26
Honolulu, Hawaii 96810
(808) 537-1868
Eleanor I. Pierce

Idaho State Bar
Post Office Box 895
Boise, Idaho 83701
(208) 342-8958
Sam F. Seever

Illinois State Bar Association
Illinois Bar Center
Springfield, Illinois 62701
(217) 525-1760
John H. Dickason

Indiana State Bar Association
230 East Ohio, 6th Floor
Indianapolis, Indiana 46204
(317) 639-5465
Jack Lyle

Iowa State Bar Association
1101 Fleming Bldg.
Des Moines, Iowa 50309
(515) 243-3179
Edward H. Jones

Kansas Bar Association
Post Office Box 1037
Topeka, Kansas 66601
(913) 234-5696
Ken Klein

Kentucky Bar Association
West Main at Kentucky River
Frankfort, Kentucky 40601
(502) 564-3795
Leslie G. Whitmer

Louisiana State Bar Association
225 Baronne Street, Suite 210
New Orleans, Louisiana 70112
(504) 566-1600
Thomas O. Collins, Jr.

Maine State Bar Association
Post Office Box 788
Augusta, Maine 04330
(207) 622-7523
Edward M. Bonney

Maryland State Bar Association, Inc.
207 East Redwood Street, Suite 905
Baltimore, Maryland 21202
(301) 685-7878
William J. Smith

Massachusetts Bar Association
One Center Plaza
Boston, Massachusetts 02108
(617) 523-4529
Carl A. Modecki

State Bar of Michigan
306 Townsend Street
Lansing, Michigan 48933
(517) 372-9030
Michael Franck

Minnesota State Bar Association
Minnesota Bar Center
430 Marquette Ave.
Minneapolis, Minnesota 55401
(612) 335-1183
Celene Green

Mississippi State Bar
620 North State Street
Jackson, Mississippi 39201
(601) 948-4471
Larry Houchins

The Missouri Bar
Post Office Box 119
Jefferson City, Missouri 65102
(314) 635-4128
Wade F. Baker

State Bar of Montana
Post Office Box 4669
Helena, Montana 59601
(406) 442-7660
Kent M. Parcell

Nebraska State Bar Association
1019 Sharp Bldg.
Lincoln, Nebraska 68508
(402) 475-7091
Ted E. Dillow

State Bar of Nevada
834 Willow Street
Reno, Nevada 89501
(702) 329-4100
J. Roger Detweiler

New Hampshire Bar Association
77 Market Street
Manchester, New Hampshire 03101
(603) 609-4869
Joseph S. Hayden

New Jersey State Bar Association
172 West State Street
Trenton, New Jersey 08608
(609) 394-1101
Dalton W. Menhall

State Bar of New Mexico
Post Office Box 25883
Albuquerque, New Mexico 87125
(505) 842-6132
Judy A. Zanotti

New York State Bar Association
One Elk Street
Albany, New York 12207
(518) 445-1211
William J. Carroll

North Carolina State Bar
Post OFfice Box 25850
Raleigh, North Carolina 27611
(919) 828-4620
B.E. James

North Carolina Bar Association
1025 Wade Avenue
Raleigh, North Carolina 27605
(919) 828-0561
William M. Storey

State Bar Association of North Dakota
Post Office Box 2136
Bismarck, North Dakota 58501
(701) 255-1404
Joel W. Gilbertson

Ohio State Bar Association
33 West 11th Avenue
Columbus, Ohio 43201
(614) 421-2121
Joseph B. Miller

Oklahoma Bar Association
Post Office Box 53036
Oklahoma City, Oklahoma 73152
(405) 524-2365
Stuart B. Strasner

Oregon State Bar
1776 S.W. Madison Street
Portland, Oregon 97205
(503) 224-4280
Robert J. Elfers

Pennsylvania Bar Association
Post Office Box 186
Harrisburg, Pennsylvania 17108
(717) 238-6715
Peter P. Roper

Puerto Rico Bar Association
Post Office Box 1900
San Juan, Puerto Rico 00903
(809) 724-3358
Carmen R. Cintron Ferrer

Rhode Island Bar Association
1804 Industrial Bank Bldg.
Providence, Rhode Island 02903
(401) 421-5740
Edward P. Smith

South Carolina Bar
Post Office Box 11039
Columbia, South Carolina 29211
(803) 799-6653
Robert N. DuRant

State Bar of South Dakota
222 East Capitol
Pierre, South Dakota 57501
(605) 224-7554
William K. Sahr

Tennessee Bar Association
3622 West End Avenue
Nashville, Tennessee 37205
(615) 383-7421
Billie Bethel

State Bar of Texas
Post Office Box 12487
Austin, Texas 78711
(512) 475-4200
Tom Hanna

Utah State Bar
425 East First South
Salt Lake City, Utah 84111
(801) 531-9077
Dean W. Sheffield

Vermont Bar Association
Post Office Box 100
Montpelier, Vermont 05602
(802) 223-2020
Lawrence J. Turgeon

Virginia State Bar
Suite 1622
700 East Main Street
Richmond, Virginia 23219
(804) 786-2061
N. Samuel Clifton

Virginia Bar Association
Post Office Box 1029
Charlottesville, Virginia 22902
(804) 977-1396
A. Ward Sims

Washington State Bar Association
505 Madison Street
Seattle, Washington 98104
(206) 622-6054
G. Edward Friar

West Virginia State Bar
E-404 State Capitol
Charleston, West Virginia 25305
(304) 346-8414
Mark P. Smith

West Virginia Bar Association
Post Office Box 346
Charleston, West Virginia 25322
(304) 342-1474
F. Witcher McCullough

State Bar of Wisconsin
Post Office Box 7158
Madison, Wisconsin 53707
(608) 257-3838
Stephen L. Smay

Wyoming State Bar
Post Office Box 3388
Cheyenne, Wyoming 82001
(307) 632-9061
William A. Taylor

INDEX OF NAMES

ABOUT THE AUTHORS

FREDERICK A. ELLISTON (PhD, Philosophy) is Senior Research Associate at the Center for the Study of Ethics in the Professions at the Illinois Institute of Technology. He specialized in phenomenology and existentialism and published books on Husserl, Heidegger and Sartre. His recent work, in professional ethics and applied philosophy, covers human sexuality, feminism, crime, the police, lawyers and whistleblowing. He published _Philosophy and Sex_, _Feminism and Philosophy_.

From 1978 to 1980 he held a fellowship in criminal justice at the State University of New York at Albany. He codirected two conferences and published the proceedings: _Ethics, Public Policy and Criminal Justice_ and _Moral Issues in Police Work_. From 1981 to 1983 he conducted a survey of courses and curricular materials that produced _Teaching Police Ethics: A Report from the the Police Foundation_. His published papers include "Women, Minorities and the Police"; "Deadly Force and Capital Punishment"; "Teaching Police Ethics"; and "Deadly Force: An Ethical Analysis". He is completing work on a reader _Ethics and the Legal Profession_ for Prometheus Books.

Under a grant from the National Science Foundation he directed a two year project on whistleblowing. The two volume report will be published late in 1984 by Praeger. He coedited a bibliography _Professional Dissent_ and is compiling a reader _Conflicting Loyalties in the Workplace_. He has published papers on anonymous whistleblowing and whistleblowing vs civil disobedience.

He is a member of the American Society of Criminologists, the Academy of Criminal Justice Sciences, the American Philosophical Association, the Hastings Center and associate editor for _Criminal Justice Ethics_ and _Applied Philosophy_.

JANE VAN SCHAICK received her B.A. from the College of St. Rose in Albany, New York, and is completing her M.B.A. at the Illinois Institute of Technology. She is currently writing a chronicle on the Quality of Work Life at Illinois Bell and planning a conference on employment of the disabled. She has also conducted research on human resource management.

Ms. van Schaick has published a bibliography on judicial ethics, _Selected Literature on Judicial Conduct and Disability: An Annotated Bibliography_ for the American Judicature Society. As Research Associate she coauthored two books with Dr. Elliston: _Whistleblowing: Managing Dissent in the Workplace_ and _Studying Whistleblowing: Methodological and Moral Issues_. She served as Project Associate on Teaching Police Ethics and helped write the final report forthcoming from the Police Foundation. Finally, she and Dr. Elliston coauthored "Whistleblowing: A Strategic Analysis", presented at the American Association for the Advancement of Science and published in _Conflicting Loyalties in the Workplace_.